The Multinational Force and Observers in the Sinai

Westview Special Studies

The concept of Westview Special Studies is a response to the continuing crisis in academic and informational publishing. Library budgets are being diverted from the purchase of books and used for data banks, computers, micromedia, and other methods of information retrieval. Interlibrary loan structures further reduce the edition sizes required to satisfy the needs of the scholarly community. Economic pressures on university presses and the few private scholarly publishing companies have greatly limited the capacity of the industry to properly serve the academic and research communities. As a result, many manuscripts dealing with important subjects, often representing the highest level of scholarship, are no longer economically viable publishing projects--or, if accepted for publication, are typically subject to lead times ranging from one to three years.

Westview Special Studies are our practical solution to the problem. As always, the selection criteria include the importance of the subject, the work's contribution to scholarship, and its insight, originality of thought, and excellence of exposition. We accept manuscripts in camera-ready form, typed, set, or word processed according to specifications laid out in our comprehensive manual, which contains straightforward instructions and sample pages. The responsibility for editing and proofreading lies with the author or sponsoring institution, but our editorial staff is always available to answer questions and provide guidance.

The result is a book printed on acid-free paper and bound in sturdy, library-quality soft covers. We manufacture these books ourselves using equipment that does not require a lengthy make-ready process and that allows us to publish first editions of 300 to 1000 copies and to reprint even smaller quantities as needed. Thus, we can produce Special Studies quickly and can keep even very specialized books in print as long as there is a demand for them.

About the Book and Author

After it became clear that the UN Security Council would not set up a peacekeeping force to fulfill the role envisaged for it in the 1979 Egyptian-Israeli Peace Treaty--supervising the implementation of the treaty and preventing any violation of its terms--the Multinational Force and Observers (MFO) was established in its place. This book provides a detailed description of the structure and function of the MFO in order to evaluate its chances for success. In addition, the author has included various documents regarding the MFO's legal basis and organization. The MFO is the first modern multinational peacekeeping force that is independent of any organization; in the future it may serve as a prototype for multinational peacekeeping forces in conflicts and areas in which the UN is unwilling or unable to become involved.

Dr. Mala Tabory is associate editor of the Israel Yearbook On Human Rights published at Tel Aviv University. During 1983-1984 she was a research Fellow at the Center for the Study of Human Rights, Columbia University.

To the sister
I never knew
NECHAMA BEILA WELTSMAN ז"ל
Born in 1938
Taken from the Lodz Ghetto
26 Elul 5702 (1942)

The Multinational Force and Observers in the Sinai
Organization, Structure, and Function

Mala Tabory

Foreword by Dr. Ruth Lapidoth

Westview Press / Boulder and London

Westview Special Studies on the Middle East

Copyright © 1986 by Westview Press, Inc.

Published in 1986 in the United States of America by Westview Press, Inc,;
Frederick A. Praeger, Publisher; 5500 Central Avenue, Boulder, Colorado 80301

Library of Congress Cataloging in Publication Data
Tabory, Mala
   The Multinational Force and Observers in the Sinai
   (Westview special studies on the Middle East)
   Bibliography: p.
   Includes index.
   1. Multinational Force and Observers. 2. Israel-Arab War, 1973--
Peace. 3. Egypt--Foreign relations--Israel. 4. Israel--Foreign
relations--Egypt. I. Title.
DS128.183.T33   1985   341.5'8   85-5319
ISBN 0-8133-0212-9

Printed and bound in the United States of America

The paper used in this publication meets the minimum requirements
of the American National Standard for Permanence of Paper for
Printed Library Materials Z39.48-1984.

10 9 8 7 6 5 4 3 2 1

Contents

Foreword

The establishment of the MFO was a remarkable phenomenon: two States (Egypt and Israel), with the help of a superpower (the United States) established a peacekeeping force without any link to an existing international organization. The force has come into being, it fulfills its functions faithfully and diligently. This phenomenon deserves a close examination, both from the political and the legal point of view. How was it established? How does it function? How is the chain of command organized? What are its legal capacities? Does it possess international personality? What is its status vis-à-vis those who participate in it? All these questions are carefully analyzed and discussed by the author.

Of course, there are no (or very few) miracles in the international arena, and there can be no doubt that despite its relative independence, the MFO could not be successful if its founders had not wished and continued to wish it to succeed. But the good will of the States involved, though a necessary condition, is not always a guarantee for the success of a peacekeeping operation. The author discusses all the elements which have contributed to the force's success.

The MFO could serve as a precedent for other situations and initiatives. Hence the special importance of the present study which will serve as a guide for those who might wish to learn from the MFO experience and consider its possible implications to other situations. In particular, the author has succeeded in comparing the advantages and disadvantages of a United Nations force with those of a force which is not connected to an international organization. Her well-balanced conclusions will be of great help to both the scholar and the practitioner in the sphere of peacekeeping.

Since I had the privilege to be personally involved in the establishment of the MFO as the legal adviser to one of the parties, I am particularly interested in Dr. Mala Tabory's research and appreciate the thoroughness and comprehensiveness of her careful analysis.

Dr. Ruth Lapidoth
Professor of International Law
The Hebrew University of Jerusalem

Acknowledgments

I am grateful to the officials and officers who patiently answered my questions and commented on successive drafts and sections of this work as events unfolded. Since most of the persons who helped me asked to remain anonymous, I thought it best not to identify anyone by name. Nevertheless, I hope that they will consider this book a tribute to their efforts and devotion. Any shortcomings or errors are, of course, solely my responsibility.

This book was developed during the 1983-84 academic year, when I was a research fellow at the Center for the Study of Human Rights of Columbia University in New York. It was written and produced in 1984-85 at the Faculty of Law of Tel Aviv University, to which I belong. I am grateful to these institutions for their assistance and support in numerous ways. It gives me pleasure to thank Mrs. Audrey Sehaik, and Mrs. Rachel Sandler, who worked to set this book on a new and awesome word processor and braved the vicissitudes of the computer. Ephie, Shlomit and Amiel were gracious in their understanding of my preoccupation with this work.

I visited the MFO North Base Camp in July 1985 as coordinator of a course for students of the Temple University Law School Summer Program on Legal Aspects of the Middle East Conflict. The briefings and our observations and conversations there served as an inspiration and as a symbol of the peace so crucial to this area.

Mala Tabory

We were starting something that had never been done,
certainly in modern history. Two countries had come
together in peace and asked an unidentified community
of nations to put together a force that would assist
in their efforts to keep peace. . . .

                                        ---L. Hunt
                                  January 17, 1983

1
Introduction

BACKGROUND

The Multinational Force and Observers in the Sinai (MFO) represents a unique and innovative effort in peacekeeping. The purpose of this book is to describe the MFO, its conception, creation, its structure and organization, its functions, duties and rights, in order to test its suitability for its assigned tasks and evaluate its chances for success.

The Middle East has been the site of various multinational forces over the past four decades, and Israel has probably had more peacekeeping forces near its borders than any other State in the world. The international forces in the region for the most part have been under the auspices of the United Nations (with the exception of the Arab League's force sent to Kuwait in mid-1961 and the Syrian-dominated Arab Deterrent Force in Lebanon created in 1976). They include UNTSO (United Nations Truce Supervision Organization, 1948 to the present), UNEF-I (United Nations Emergency Force, 1956-1967), UNEF-II (1974-1979), UNDOF (United Nations Disengagement Observer Force, 1974 to the present), UNIFIL (United Nations Interim Force in Lebanon, 1978 to the present), UNOGIL (United Nations Observer Group in Lebanon, 1958), and UNYOM (United Nations Yemen Observation Mission, 1963-1964).

Following years of conflict, Egypt and Israel set forth the security arrangements for the Sinai and the Negev along their common border in the Peace Treaty of March 26, 1979.[1] The Peace Treaty stipulates that the Sinai be divided into three Zones --

1

identified as A, B and C (see Map in Appendix). In the westernmost Zone A, bounded on the west by the Gulf of Suez and the Suez Canal, Egypt is permitted a limited number of armed forces, weapons and armored vehicles. The limitation increases progressively eastward, and in the easternmost Zone C, parallel to the international border and the Egyptian shore of the Gulf of Aqaba (Eilat) and on the Islands of Tiran and Sanafir, no Egyptian forces may be stationed except for Egyptian civil police. As a measure of reciprocity and formal equality between the parties, a narrow Zone D of up to three kilometers wide was established on the Israeli side of the international border, in which Israeli military personnel and equipment are limited.

This comprehensive arrangement understandably engendered sensitivities on the part of both Egypt and Israel. Israel was handing the Sinai over to Egypt in return for its partial demilitarization as part of an overall security arrangement between the two parties. Perhaps in deference to Egyptian sensitivities over its sovereignty in the Sinai, the term "limitation of forces" was preferred over "demilitarization." Legally, however, as pointed out by Professor Ruth Lapidoth, demilitarization -- namely the limitation of forces on the basis of a treaty between the parties -- does not have the effect of curtailing sovereignty.[2]

The complete withdrawal by Israel from the Sinai was contingent upon the establishment of guarantees of satisfactory security arrangements, as set forth in the 1979 Egyptian-Israeli Peace Treaty. According to the Treaty, the parties agreed to the stationing of UN personnel in the area to supervise aspects of its implementation and to prevent any violation of its terms.[3] In the framework of the peace process, the short-range intermediate purpose of the force to be established was to supervise the withdrawal, and its long-range purposes were to guarantee the implementation of the permanent security arrangements and to ensure freedom of navigation in the Strait of Tiran.

Already in March 1979 it became clear that the USSR might prevent the participation of the UN in the implementation of the Peace Treaty, due to its opposition to the Treaty as a whole and to her own lack of participation in the peace process. Therefore, upon Israel's request, the United States, in an identical letter to the parties dated March 26, 1979, which forms part of the "treaty package," agreed that if the UN Security Council failed to establish and maintain the arrangements called for in the Treaty, the US President would "be prepared to take those steps necessary to ensure the establishment and maintenance of an acceptable alternative multinational force."[4] This was indeed what happened, as the UN was unable and unwilling to play an active role in the framework of the Peace Treaty.[5]

On July 24, 1979, when the mandate for the United Nations Emergency Force (UNEF-II), which fulfilled various functions by virtue of the disengagement agreements, was up for renewal, the Security Council did not extend its stay in the Sinai where the Force had been functioning since 1974. This was because of the negative attitude of the USSR.[6] The Soviet position apparently was that the United Nations Truce Supervision Organization (UNTSO), "as the permanent UN peacekeeping mission in the area, could supervise the Israeli withdrawal in fulfillment of Security Council resolution 242, without involving the United Nations in the implementation of the peace treaty itself."[7]

The United States and the Soviet Union reached an understanding regarding the role of UNTSO. They "obtained the rather clandestine approval of the Security Council for the employment of UNTSO observers in supervising the execution of the treaty."[8] The proposal of UN Secretary-General, Kurt Waldheim, that the supervisory function be carried out by UNTSO, was rejected by Israel. It pointed out that, as a party directly involved, it had not even been consulted regarding such an arrangement.[9]

Israel strongly objected to UNTSO. Its position was that observers were not a suitable substitute for a force, and that UNTSO was inherently incapable of performing the functions allotted to the "forces and observers" under the Peace Treaty. As soon as it became evident that the UN would not play any role in the implementation of the Peace Treaty, the question of UNTSO became moot.

INTERIM SUPERVISORY PROCEDURES

In concrete terms, the question of an alternative to a UN force arose as early as May 1979, when Israel returned El Arish and the north-eastern Sinai coastal strip to Egypt.[10] According to the Peace Treaty, UN forces were to enter immediately the areas evacuated by the withdrawing Israeli forces in order to establish interim and temporary buffer zones, for the purpose of maintaining a separation of forces. The deployment of UN forces was to precede the movement of any other personnel into such areas. Only within seven days after Israeli withdrawal were units of the Egyptian armed forces or border units to deploy in evacuated areas.[11]

Since the UN was unwilling to cooperate, Egypt and Israel agreed to direct transfers, and there were joint military ceremonies on these occasions. These direct transfers without an intermediary, effected due to the lack of an alternative force to fill the void, represented an act of good faith on the part of Israel. It was a complicated undertaking, requiring the coordination of one army withdrawing and another taking over, with the latter having to be acquainted with water facilities, installations, etc., in the field in a short time.

According to the Peace Treaty, on January 25, 1980 (nine months from the date of exchange of the instruments of ratification), Israel was to withdraw, as the first phase, to the El Arish-Ras Muhammed line,[12] and the UN forces and observers were to supervise the withdrawal.[13]

It was envisaged in the Peace Treaty that a five-kilometer wide interim buffer zone, by which the UN force would effect a separation of Egyptian and Israeli elements, would be established west of and adjacent to the El Arish-Ras Muhammed interim withdrawal line. The UN force was to have operated checkpoints, reconnaissance patrols, and observation posts within this interim buffer zone in order to supervise limitation of armaments and movement of Israeli personnel in the four military technical installations operated by Israel.[14]

Prior to the completion of the first phase of withdrawal, Israel had asked the US to fulfill its promise of establishing an alternate multinational force. The American reply was that it would act on its obligation only if the UN refused to become involved towards the end of the period prior to Israel's final withdrawal from the Sinai, i.e., in April 1982. Moreover, the US maintained that States could not be found who were willing to participate in a non-UN force. Nevertheless, in order not to leave the area without supervisory arrangements, representatives of Israel, Egypt and the US met in Washington in September 1979 and agreed upon alternative supervisory procedures. These consisted of (a) in the interim buffer zone, joint Egyptian-Israeli supervision; (b) in the remaining areas evacuated by Israel, supervision by the Sinai Field Mission (SFM); and (c) US airborne surveillance flights over Sinai.

(a) Egyptian-Israeli Supervision

At the time that Israel was to hand over to Egypt the Sinai up to the El Arish-Ras Muhammed line, there was no supervisory force. Egypt was freely receiving a substantial portion of the Sinai as prescribed by the Peace Treaty, without there being an outside force to fulfill the security functions stipulated in the Treaty. Thus, in this regard, too, Israel demonstrated its good faith.

In practice, in the absence of a separating element, the interim buffer zone turned into a line of contact between the parties, with joint supervision by Israeli-Egyptian groups. This included Egyptian checkpoints on the eastern line of the Zone, Israeli checkpoints on the western line of the Zone, and joint supervision through observation posts and patrols in between. This was achieved by joint checkpoints (CPs) and Buffer Observation and Reconnaissance units (BORs), eight or nine each. These arrangements were not all embodied in binding written agreements, due to some disagreements between the parties on certain points, but they were carried out in practice.[15]

(b) Sinai Field Mission (SFM) Supervision

Since a new UN force was not yet established at that time, and the USSR refused to extend the mandate of UNEF-II, while Israel rejected the use of UNTSO observers to implement the Peace Treaty, it was agreed that the US Sinai Field Mission (SFM), instead of being disbanded -- as stipulated in the Peace Treaty -- in January 1980, would continue to monitor the Sinai Peninsula (within its authorized limit of up to 200 persons).

Israel's suggestion regarding the role of the SFM was accepted by Egypt and by the US President and Congress.[16] Its role was more symbolic than instrumental, as the SFM at that time consisted only of some 30 to 40 observers.

The US Sinai Field Mission, established in 1976 in accordance with the Agreement between Egypt and Israel of September 1, 1975 [second disengagement agreement], consisted of up to 200 US civilians charged with monitoring the electronic early warning stations around the strategic Gidi and Mitla passes and inspecting the parties' surveillance stations.[17] The SFM was well liked by the parties, fulfilled its functions successfully and had worked well alongside UNEF-II. In the Peace Treaty, the parties requested the US operated Sinai Field Mission to continue its operations until the completion of the Israeli withdrawal from the area east of the Gidi and Mitla Passes (which the SFM monitored). It was envisaged that the SFM would then be terminated.[18]

In fact, it was agreed that the SFM would continue to operate for no longer than the three-year period of the Israeli withdrawal. It converted its task from electronic surveillance to limited verification of the security arrangements in the Sinai, including the monitoring of military technical installations operated by Israel in the buffer zone, and only ceased to function as an entity in April 1982. Some of its observers were then hired by the MFO on the basis of individual contracts, and thus those persons function as part of the observer group of the MFO.

(c) US Air Surveillance

In the Peace Treaty the parties also requested the US to continue airborne surveillance flights in accordance with previous agreements (i.e. the Agreement between Egypt and Israel of 1975) until the completion of the final Israeli withdrawal.[19] The three provisional security arrangements ended with the completion of the withdrawal. As described below, special provisions were later made for US air surveillance flights to continue, in the same format and manner as previously, as part of the supervision of the permanent security arrangements.

These procedures, which covered most, but not all, of the tasks envisaged for the UN force according to the Peace Treaty, were sufficient as regards the areas evacuated during the first phase. However, they did not provide a solution for the area 20 to 50 kilometers west of the international border, where UN forces were to have been deployed in the final phase. Israel made it clear already in September 1979 that she was not willing to give in on this matter, and suggested two alternatives: either supervision by joint Israeli-Egyptian forces, as in the interim buffer zone, or setting up a multinational force. Egypt rejected the first suggestion, as she was sensitive to the issue of sovereignty over Sinai and considered this an attempt by Israel to reenter the area "through the back door." Therefore the US was asked to stand by its commitment and establish an alternative multinational force.[20]

In light of the inability of the UN to provide a force, and the requirements for such a force to implement the Peace Treaty, it was necessary to devise a new force ex nihilo. Novelty of conception and creativeness in organization were required to achieve this. The result of this effort is the Multinational Force and Observers (MFO).

NOTES

(1) Treaty of Peace between the State of Israel and the Arab Republic of Egypt. Text in 18 Int'l Legal Materials 362 (1979) (hereinafter: Peace Treaty).

(2) See Ruth Lapidoth, "The Multinational Force and Observers in the Sinai and the Negev" (Hebrew), in Sefer Sussman 369-88, at 370 (Gavriela Shalev ed. Jerusalem 1984) (hereinafter: Lapidoth).

(3) Peace Treaty, Art. 4 and Agreed Minutes thereto; Annex I, Art. 6; Appendix to Annex I, Arts. 3, 5.

(4) 15 Is. L. Rev. 322 (1980).

(5) The only roles fulfilled by the UN since the conclusion of the Peace Treaty were: the withdrawal of UN troops from Western Sinai (a small number of UNTSO observers continue to hold a small number of posts in the Sinai, with Egypt's consent), and hosting the first session of the Joint Israel-Egypt Commission at the UN base at Tassa on April 29, 1979, without taking any active role in that meeting. "The Multinational Force" (Hebrew), Ma'arachot (No. 283) 27 (July 1982).

(6) UN Doc. S/13468, July 24, 1979. On UNEF-II see Nissim Bar-Yaacov, "Keeping the Peace between Egypt and Israel, 1973-1980," 15 Is. L. Rev. 197 (1980). On the Soviet position see ibid., 250-51; Richard W. Nelson, "Multinational Peacekeeping in the Middle East and the United Nations Model," 61 Int'l Aff. (London) 67, at 68 (Winter 1984-85).

(7) On UNTSO see Rosalyn Higgins, United Nations Peacekeeping 1946-1967 -- Documents and Commentary, Vol. I: The Middle East 5-217 (Oxford 1969). Michael Comay, "UN Peacekeeping: The Israeli Experience," in Peacekeeping: Appraisals & Proposals 93-117, at 99 (Henry Wiseman ed. N.Y. 1983); Bar-Yaacov, supra note 6, at 202ff.

(8) Bar-Yaacov, supra note 6, at 198-99.

(9) Comay, supra note 7.

(10) Peace Treaty, Appendix to Annex I, Art. 2, para. 1(a): "First subphase: within two months, Israeli armed forces will withdraw from the area of El Arish, including the town of El Arish and its airfield, shown as Area I on Map 3."

(11) Ibid., Art. 1, para. 2 (c-e).

(12) Peace Treaty, Annex I, Art. 1, para. 3(a): "The interim withdrawal behind the line from east of El Arish to Ras Muhammed as delineated on Map 2 within nine months from the date of exchange of instruments of ratification of this Treaty." See Map 2 in Appendix.

(13) Ibid., Annex I, Art. 6, para. 1: "The Parties will request the United Nations to provide forces and observers to supervise the implementation of this Annex..."

(14) Peace Treaty, Appendix to Annex I, Art. 5.

(15) Lapidoth, p. 371. See Ma'arachot, supra note 5, at 27.

(16) See Bar-Yaacov, supra note 6, at 257-61.

(17) UN Doc. S/11818/Add.1, Sept. 2, 1975; also 14 Int'l Legal Materials 1450 (1975).   See Bar-Yaacov, supra note 6, at 226-35. N.A. Pelcovits, Security Guarantees in a Middle East Settlement 10 (Sage Policy Paper No. 5, 1976).

(18) Peace Treaty, Appendix to Annex I, Art. 7, para. 2. See US letter dated March 26, 1979, accompanying Peace Treaty (supra note 4).

(19) Peace Treaty, Appendix to Annex I, Art. 7, para. 1(a).

(20) Ma'arachot, supra note 5, at 28.   The possibility of introducing foreign forces from outside the Middle East in Arab territory, as an alternative likely to meet with less resistance than would be raised by the stationing of Israeli forces is mentioned by Uri Bialer, in "Military Forces within Foreign Territory under Peace Arrangements -- Ramifications of 20th Century Historic Experience upon Possible Arrangements between Israel and Arab Countries," 17 J. Peace Research 47, at 58 (1980).

2
Establishment of the MFO: Chronology

This chapter describes the sequence of key events leading to the establishment of the MFO. It demonstrates the intricate diplomatic maneuvers that were required to secure the agreement of the host and participant States in the MFO.

In February 1981 the US began to work on the establishment of a multinational force, and talks to that end were initiated. Egypt insisted that an effort first be made to request the UN Security Council to constitute the required force. Therefore some attempts were made early in 1981 to secure a post-withdrawal UN force and observers, as called for in the Peace Treaty. However, on May 18, 1981, in response to a formal request from the Permanent Representative of Egypt (dated April 21, 1981), the President of the Security Council confirmed that the Council members had been unable to reach the necessary agreement regarding the establishment of a UN force.[1] Egypt and Israel, with the help of the US, then began negotiating an agreement to serve as the basis for establishing a multinational force and observer group outside the framework of the UN. During the period of the negotiations, teams were formed to plan construction and logistics, list the force's eventual personnel and equipment requirements, and to formulate recommendations for the recruitment of national contingents and the nomination of senior officials.

On July 17, 1981, representatives of Egypt (Ambassador Taher Shash) and Israel (David Kimche, Director General of the Israeli Foreign Ministry), together with Ambassador Michael Sterner, Deputy Assistant Secretary of State for Near Eastern and South Asian

11

Affairs, representing the US, met at the US embassy in London and initialed a protocol and related documents regarding the establishment and functions of the Multinational Force and Observers in the Sinai (MFO), as an alternative to the force provided in the Egypt-Israel Peace Treaty.[2] The Protocol was formally signed by Egyptian Ambassador to the US Ashraf A. Gorbal and Israeli Ambassador to the US Ephraim Evron at a ceremony at the Department of State on August 3, 1981, and was witnessed by Secretary of State Alexander M. Haig, Jr., on behalf of the US Government.[3]

On July 17, 1981, a letter was sent to the US confirming Egypt and Israel's agreement to appoint Mr. Leamon R. Hunt to act as interim Director-General of the MFO, pending the entry into force of the Protocol establishing the MFO initialed on the same day. The parties empowered Mr. Hunt "to take the necessary steps to ensure that preparations for the deployment of the MFO in accordance with the Protocol are initiated in a timely fashion." Each Government made available to the interim Director-General $20 million upon which he could draw for that purpose. The interim Director-General was to cease to function upon the appointment of a Director-General, or on October 1, 1981, whichever came first.[4]

On July 23, 1981, the US, in separate notes, informed the parties that following the final Israeli withdrawal from Sinai and "subject to Congressional authorization and appropriation," the US would continue air surveillance flights in Egypt over Zones A, B and C and in Israel over Zone D (see map). These notes were the product of lengthy negotiations that took place simultaneously with the negotiations over the MFO Protocol. It was felt that these flights, which according to the Peace Treaty were to have been discontinued after Israel's final withdrawal to the international border, should be continued in view of the fact that there would not be a UN force and that supervisory functions would fall on an alternative US-backed force.[5] Positive replies were received from Egypt and Israel at the end of July.[6] The acceptance of the US notes on this subject by Egypt and Israel respectively constituted an "arrangement" on the conduct of air surveillance over the designated areas.[7]   Both sides agreed that US flights would continue once a week.   It was decided that until the withdrawal to the interim withdrawal line, the US would not provide the actual aerial photographs, but only their interpretation. (This had been the procedure since the period when Ezer Weizman served as Israeli Defense Minister.) In practice, this arrangement was then continued, with US aerial coverage of all four Zones.[8]   The implication is that the parties, instead of receiving aerial photographs, are provided only with information and conclusions by the US based on these photographs regarding compliance with the terms of the Treaty and whether there are any violations.

On August 3, 1981, the US sent identical letters to Egypt and Israel confirming and spelling out the US role in the establishment and functioning of the MFO.   Secretary of State Alexander Haig proposed that his letters and the replies thereto constitute an agreement among the three States; Israel and Egypt agreed to this.[9]   This agreement, along with the others mentioned above, had already been initialed on July 17.

On September 26, 1981, the UN declared its unwillingness to back the MFO.

On October 20, 1981, US President Reagan asked Congress to appropriate $10 million to fund the posting of American Observers in the Sinai peninsula stationed there since 1976 until the completion of the next stage of the Camp David Accords.

By late summer of 1981, the essential political, administrative and financial structure of the MFO was in place. The basic military structure of the Force had been decided upon, although final agreements on contingent participation had not been completed.   "The diplomats and planners had completed their phase of the creation of the new organization, and passed their work to the logisticians and builders."[10]

On November 15 talks began in Cairo between the Egyptian Foreign Minister, Kamal Hassan Ali, the Director-General of the MFO, Leamon Hunt, and the Military Commander, Norwegian Lieutenant-General Frederik Bull-Hansen.   The discussions were conducted in Israel between November 16 and 20.   The negotiations dealt with the structure, location, equipment and functions of the force.

Fiji and then Colombia each had agreed in the summer of 1981 to contribute a battalion to the MFO.

The US Congress moved slowly to authorize US participation in the MFO. On October 7, 1981, the Senate (by a voice vote) approved a resolution authorizing the assignment of up to 1200 US troops to the MFO.[11] On November 19 the House of Representatives passed a slightly different version of the Sinai force resolution.[12]

On November 22, 1981, France, Great Britain, Italy and Holland (the "four" European powers) first announced their agreement to participate in the MFO. (Due to the intricacy of attitudes, motives and conditions involved in securing European participation in the Force, this aspect is described separately below.) On the following day, individual supplementary statements were issued by the Four, as well as a statement by the Ten Community States. On November 27, 1981, against the background of Israel's threatening to veto European participation in the force because of statements by the governments of the European "Four" on the Arab-Israeli dispute that in Israel's view seemed irrelevant to the issue under consideration, US Secretary of State Alexander M. Haig, Jr., and Israeli Foreign Minister Yitzhak Shamir met for seven-and-a-half hours to try to smooth things over, apparently with success.[13]

On December 3, 1981, the US and Israel issued a joint statement on European participation in the MFO (text infra). On the same day the Israeli Cabinet accepted the joint US-Israeli statement ackowledging the divergent views on Arab-Israeli issues, but noted that the four European States had attached "no political conditions" to their participation in the Sinai Force.

On December 29, 1981, President Reagan signed into law, as Public Law No. 97-132, legislation authorizing US participation in the MFO.[14]

During December 1981 and January 1982, operational planning and the drafting of the future standing operating procedures for the Force took place in Alexandria, Virginia, the MFO's temporary headquarters, with the participation of military officers from various nations who would later form the nucleus of Lieutenant-

General Bull-Hansen's staff. On December 28 an important meeting took place between MFO officials, an Egyptian delegation (headed by Rear-Admiral Mohsen Hamdy) and an Israeli delegation (headed by Brigadier-General Dov Sion, later respectively their country's closest link with the MFO), during which the Director-General presented the MFO's completed operational concept, and additional discussions focused on force organization and future plans.[15]

On February 15, 1982, the Director-General of the MFO and the Commander of the Force reported to Israel Defense Minister Ariel Sharon on the progress in constituting the Force. The ten contributing States at that time were selecting and training their contingents. (Three contingents were ready at that time: the US, Colombia and Fiji.)

On March 10, the MFO started deploying troops in the Sinai. Force Commander Bull-Hansen and his staff were on location to supervise operational arrangements and welcome arriving contingents. By March 20, as required by the Protocol,[16] all contingents were in place, ready for orientation and training. On that day, Bull-Hansen issued his Day Order No. 1, asking his troops to do their "utmost to maintain the integrity, impartiality and independence of our multinational organization."[17]

The Force trained and organized itself to take on the peacekeeping duty and carry out reconnaissance. According to schedule, the MFO was to assume its functions at 1300 hours on April 25, 1982.[18] This was indeed the case, as Israel withdrew from the Sinai on that day. At a ceremony at El Gorah, which that day became the MFO's Sinai headquarters, the Sinai was returned to Egyptian sovereignty and the MFO began its mission. Soldiers took up their new duties in Zone C, and the civilian observers prepared for their first verification missions.

It is to the credit of the United States that the MFO was effectively constituted in a relatively short time. This was thanks to the work of advance teams and "fast track" construction, permitting simultaneous design, procurement and construction.[19]

The MFO Protocol formally entered into force on February 3,

1983, the date on which Israel notified Egypt, in accordance with Article 9, that all its constitutional requirements in this regard had been fulfilled. Thus, in effect, the agreement became binding de jure almost a year after the Force began to function de facto. Egypt's notification had been given on August 30, 1981. The Egyptian Foreign Ministry sent a formal notice to the Israeli Foreign Ministry stating that the procedure on its part was completed, based on a presidential decree. The simplified procedure in Article 9 requires only notification by each party "that all its constitutional requirements have been fulfilled," rather than the exchange of instruments of ratification.

Registration with the UN of the agreements relating to the MFO was effected on October 21, 1983. Besides the MFO Protocol, the documentation, submitted for registration by Israel, includes the Letter Agreement concerning the appointment by Egypt and Israel of the Interim Director-General, of July 17, 1981, which came into force by signature on that date; the Exchanges of Notes constituting an agreement concerning air surveillance flights provided by the US, which entered into force on July 31, 1981; the Exchange of Letters constituting an agreement concerning the US role in the establishment and maintenance of the MFO, August 3, 1981, which entered into force on that date; and the Exchange of Letters constituting an agreement concerning the authority of the Director-General of the MFO to enter into agreements with participating States in the MFO, which came into force on March 15, 1982.[20]

NOTES

(1) Creation of the Multinational Force and Observers (MFO) for the Sinai, Hearings and Markup before the Committee on Foreign Affairs and its Subcommittees on International Security and Scientific Affairs and on Europe and the Middle East, House of Representatives, 97th Congress, First Sess., on H.J. Res. 349, July 21, 28, and October 27, 1981, p. 58; text at 136 (U.S. Government Printing Office, Washington, 1981, No. 86-5330) (hereinafter: MFO House Hearings).

(2)   Text of Protocol in 81 US Dept. State Bull. (No. 2054) 44 (Sept. 1981); 20 Int'l Legal Materials 1190 (1981) (hereinafter: MFO Protocol, MFO Annex, MFO Appendix).

(3)   Marian Nash Leich, "The Sinai Multinational Force and Observers," 76 Am. J. Int'l L. 181-82 (1982). The Egyptian Parliament ratified the Protocol on August 14, as did Israel's Knesset (Parliament) earlier (see Tenth Knesset, stenographic record, 1st Sess., 3rd Mtg., pp. 4-55, July 27, 1981) (to appear in Divrei Haknesset), prior to the formal signature.

(4)   Letter from Yitzhak Shamir, Israel Minister for Foreign Affairs to US Secretary of State Alexander Haig, 26 Kitvei Amana (Israel Treaty Series) (No. 896), p. 658.

(5)   Peace Treaty, Appendix to Annex I, Art. 7, para. 1 (a). Lapidoth, p. 373. This was intended to cover only the period of withdrawal.

(6)   Texts in 26 Kitvei Amana (No. 896), pp. 659, 660.

(7)   This arrangement,from a legal standpoint, qualifies as an agreement (see Lapidoth, p. 373).

(8)   MFO House Hearings, pp. 48-49, 128.   Interviews with MFO official and with liaison officer.

(9)   Text in 20 Int'l Legal Materials (No. 5) 1190 (Sept. 1981); 26 Kitvei Amana (No. 896), pp. 663-65.

(10) Multinational Force and Observers, Annual Report of the Director General 12 (Rome, April 25, 1983) (hereinafter: MFO Annual Report, 1983).

(11) S.J. Res. 100; Background, 39 Congressional Quarterly, Weekly Report (No. 43) 2057; also 1353 (Oct. 24, 1981).   See Hearing before the Committee on Foreign Relations on S.J. Res. 100: A Joint Resolution to Authorize the Participation of the United States in a Multinational Force and Observers to Implement the Treaty of Peace between Egypt and Israel; US Senate, 97th Congress, First Sess., July 20, 1981 (U.S.   Government Printing Office, Washington, 1982, No. 82-4680) (hereinafter: MFO Senate Hearings).

(12) H.J. Res. 349; the vote was 368-13, Vote 309, Nov. 19, 1981; 39 Congressional Quarterly, Weekly Report (No. 47) 2309 (Nov. 21, 1981).   The House resolution placed a limit of 1,200 on the number of US military personnel that could be assigned to the force.   The bill also authorized the US share of the costs of the Sinai mission.   The House resolution authorized $125 million in addition to the $10 million already spent.   The House resolution required the President to send Congress reports by April 30, 1982, and by Jan. 15 of each succeeding year describing:
- The activities and composition of the force.
- All US costs in contributing to the force.
- The results of discussions with Egypt and Israel regarding the future of the Sinai force and its possible elimination or reduction.
39 Congressional Quarterly, Weekly Report (No. 49) 2415 (Dec. 5, 1981).

(13) Ibid.

(14) Text in 1 U.S. Code Congressional and Administrative News, 97th Congress, 1st Sess. (1981), p. 95 Stat. 1693; background

18

at 3 ibid., 2470. See 17 Weekly Compilation of Presidential
Documents (No. 53), Presidential Statement, Dec. 29, pp. 1428-29
(Dec. 31, 1981).

(15) MFO Annual Report, 1983, pp. 25-26.

(16) MFO Annex, Art. 34.

(17) For details on deployment, see MFO Annual Report,
1983, p. 26. For the arrival of US troops see Newsweek, March 29,
1982, p. 27; Ma'ariv (Israeli daily newspaper, Hebrew), March 17,
1982, p. 7; ibid., March 18, 1982, p. 1.

(18) MFO Annex, Art. 35.

(19) MFO Annual Report, 1983, pp. 13-14.

(20) UN Ref. LA 41 TR/211083, Nov. 4, 1983. Nos. 22403,
22404-22407, UN Statement of Treaties and International Agreements
registered or filed and recorded during the month of October 1983,
pp. 617-18.

3
Participation in the MFO

BACKGROUND

The Peace Treaty stipulates that the force will be drawn from nations (1) to be agreed upon by the parties, and (2) other than those which are Permanent Members of the UN Security Council.[1] Once it became clear that the UN would not establish a force, the limitation on the participation of the US (as well as the other Permanent Members of the Security Council) became irrelevant. Israel insisted that the US send troops, as she considered this a physical manifestation consistent with the US political commitment for the MFO's effective and continued existence. (The actual problem of withdrawal of the force is dealt with separately in a later chapter.)

Israel's insistence on US participation was based on policy considerations that (a) it was important that the force be militarily effective; (b) US financial support of the force would lighten the overall burden; and (c) the force would serve as a visible demonstration that the US political backing for the security arrangement was now embodied in the force.

While Israel strongly insisted that the force be comprised mainly of American units, Egypt preferred a multinational force. Both Israel and Egypt were interested in US participation, though Egypt was wary of an increased US presence.[2]

According to the MFO Protocol, the composition of the force was to be designated with the agreement of the two parties.[3]

This provision was of great importance in gaining the confidence of the parties in the force. "In the event of differences of view between the parties over the composition of the MFO, the two sides will invite the United States to join them in resolving any issues."[4] Subject to the authorization of the parties, the Director-General was to request those nations agreeable to the parties to supply contingents to the MFO.[5]

CONSTITUTING THE FORCE

Originally there was reluctance on the part of many suitable States to participate in the MFO. As pointed out by Pijpers, the task of constituting the force turned out to be more difficult than the peacekeeping operation itself.[6]

A variety of concerns and difficulties underlined the decision on the part of States regarding their possible participation in the MFO. For example, some States are constitutionally forbidden to contribute troops to non-UN organizations, while many were deeply concerned with a non-UN organization assuming responsibilities in the peacekeeping field which since World War II had been traditionally those of the UN.

Neither Egypt nor Israel wanted contributors from the Soviet sphere. Israel was unwilling to accept troops from States with which it does not maintain diplomatic relations. Egypt was opposed to the inclusion of African participants in order to avoid divisiveness in the OAU about the Camp David Accords.[7]

The US was concerned over the lack of response on the part of UN Member States to commit troops to the MFO, and was anxious to encourage the participation of other nations, in order to render the MFO impartial and effective. To that end, the US tried to demonstrate its total commitment to the MFO and the peace process and to encourage developed nations to follow its example. It offered incentives to developing nations in the form of US military training of the armed forces of such nations participating in the

MFO, in the hope that this would increase the desirability of their contributing forces.[8]

The US played a crucial role in recruiting participating States for the MFO. The various States did not join because of Israeli or Egyptian solicitation, but primarily because they were asked to do so by the US. US facilities were used generously in the process. Initially, negative responses came from the Nordic countries (Finland, Denmark, Norway) to participate in a force that was not under UN control. Australia and New Zealand said that the chances of their participating in the MFO were slim because of the assassination of President Anwar Sadat (October 6, 1981). This event underscored arguments by opponents of the force that the Middle East was too unstable for Australia and New Zealand to commit troops for a peacekeeping force.

Fiji, Colombia and Uruguay were the first three countries to agree to participate in the MFO. Fiji and Colombia, both of which had past experience in Middle East peacekeeping with the UN, each agreed to supply an infantry battalion (about 500 soldiers each). Uruguay offered a motor transport unit.[9]

In a letter dated August 3, 1981, sent to Egypt and Israel, and intended to constitute an agreement between the three States, the US committed itself to the following contributions to the MFO:

1. The post of Director-General is to be held by US nationals suggested by the United States. [He is actually appointed by the Egyptians and Israelis.]
2. "Subject to Congressional authorization and appropriations," the US would contribute an infantry battalion (about 750-800 soldiers) and a logistics support unit from its armed forces, as well as a group of civilian observers.[10] [The US actually recruits the observers for the MFO, which pays them and whose employees they are.]

Thus at a fairly early stage the MFO could count on the three infantry battalions (within the 2000 man limitation stipulated in Protocol Annex, Art. 19) required to man the observation posts and checkpoints in Zone C, as well as observers to monitor Treaty provisions throughout the four Zones.

It was then necessary to recruit other States to provide a broader political basis for the Force, as well as specialized support. For example, contingents with a naval patrol capability were required for the Strait of Tiran, and technical skills and capital equipment were needed to sustain operations in the field.

Israeli Foreign Minister Yitzhak Shamir canvassed the foreign ministers of France, Italy and Australia for their countries' participation in the MFO during his meetings with fellow diplomats at the UN General Assembly in September 1981.[11] The US and Egypt requested the European countries to send a symbolic contribution to the MFO, as a European gesture. In response, the Community States engaged in intensive consultations on whether to participate in the MFO. The Community countries had previously decided that they would reach a common decision, and if it were positive, the soldiers sent would probably be French and British.

Once the European Communities agreed in principle late in 1981 to participate in the MFO, talks were conducted in various EC and British Commonwealth nations which resulted in concrete contributions. Italy agreed to provide and man three coastal patrol vessels; Australia and New Zealand would supply a combined helicopter squadron; France -- an air transport unit operating two light passenger aircraft and one transport aircraft; the Netherlands -- military police and communication units; and the United Kingdom -- a headquarters unit.

The agreements, as called for in the Protocol, also related to the provision of staff officers from each contributing State to man the Force Commander's multinational staff.[12]

The European Communities' decision to participate in the MFO, of which the political and diplomatic underpinnings are not yet entirely clear, is treated separately below.

THE EUROPEAN COMMUNITIES' DECISION

European participation in the Force was considered to be important for a number of reasons. As explained by Pijpers, regarding the US:

> Firstly to commit EC countries by means of their physical presence in the Sinai, to a peace process which until then they had only supported with many reservations. Secondly, to pre-empt further European initiatives along the lines set out in Venice, which Washington considered, with some justification, competititive to its own efforts and harmful to the Camp David process. The US undoubtedly reckoned that a visible European commitment to the Camp David Accords in the Sinai would restrict Europe's special relations with the Arab world and so reduce its options in the Arab-Israeli conflict. Finally, there was the aim of cementing, at a time of increasing East-West tension, a more unified and consistent Western policy towards the Middle East, under US leadership.

Israel perhaps considered "a broad European participation as a means of legitimizing the separate peace."[13]

On October 19, 1981, French President François Mitterand announced that his Government was considering participating in the MFO. It was expected that the French decision would pave the way in influencing other European States such as Italy and perhaps Britain (and Australia in its wake) that heretofore had avoided taking part in any arrangement stemming from the Camp David Accords. (Foreign Minister Cheysson stated that the annexation of the Golan Heights by Israel would not influence his country's firm decision to participate in the MFO.)[14]

Australian and New Zealand participation in the MFO was closely linked to the European position, and it was clear that these two States would not join without the Europeans. Following the French announcement, Australian Prime Minister Malcolm Fraser stated that his country's decision regarding participation in the MFO might be influenced by the French position. Fraser told his Parliament on October 22, 1981, that Australia would participate in the MFO provided that Canada and Britain did likewise. He wanted to see European involvement in the MFO, prior to making an Australian commitment: "European participation is a critical factor. We are glad to see from published reports that France is reconsidering her attitude." He said that once Canada and Britain were included in the Force, Australia would offer transportation for the Force.[15] Fraser criticized the Europeans for the difficult conditions they set for their participation in the MFO. In his view Britain set such stringent conditions for her participation that Israel would be unable to accept them.[16] Shadow Minister of Foreign Affairs Lionel Bowen denounced Australian participation in the Sinai Force and tried to frustrate the mounting of such a force. Previously he set out to show that a multinational (as distinct from a UN) force in Sinai would be illegal under international law.

New Zealand decided in principle to send army units to the MFO on condition that Australia stood by its plan to participate in the Force. Prime Minister Robert Muldoon stated that he was not concerned about his country's commercial relations with Arab countries.[17]

The Foreign Office in London announced it was deliberating whether to join the Force, but any contribution would be modest. British readiness to join was contingent upon agreement by the Ten Community Members to a formula tying participation in the Force to progress in reaching a comprehensive Middle East peace settlement.[18] The European diplomats' favored approach appeared to be the EC's encouragement of some form of the eight-point Saudi peace plan.

The Netherlands Government announced that it was seriously considering the participation of Dutch units in the MFO. The Dutch Foreign and Defense Ministers were considering how the Netherlands might contribute to the MFO, in view of the fact that their country already had 800 men in the UNIFIL force in Lebanon.[19]

On October 26, 1981, French Foreign Minister Cheysson

announced that Italy, France, Britain and the Netherlands were considering participation. At that point, however, many obstacles stood in the way, as described below.

Italy was the first EC country to announce officially that it would join the MFO.[20] Its early decision to participate in the MFO aroused sharp criticism in Leftist and other circles.[21] Foreign Minister Colombo, speaking before the Italian Senate on November 11 during a debate on foreign policy, gave three reasons for Italy's decision to participate in the MFO:

1. In the absence of a multinational force, Israel would not withdraw from the Sinai, would fail to fulfill the Camp David Accords, and would cause chain reactions that would upset the present balance of "no-peace no-war." In other words, the multinational force would deprive Israel of an excuse for violating the Camp David Accords and for the ensuing turmoil in the Middle East. It may be that Colombo in this way sought to warn Israel lest it reject European participation, for only Israel would then be to blame for the deterioration of the situation.[22]

2. Italy, like other Community countries, perceives the Camp David Accords, which it supports, as an agreement closely linked with UN Security Council Resolution 242 (1967) calling for Israeli withdrawal from occupied territories, and the Venice Declaration -- as complementing and expanding it. (The 1980 European Community Declaration known as the Venice Declaration requires guarantees for Israel's existence and security, and at the same time first recognized the rights of the Palestinian people to self-determination.)[23]

3. The participation of the Four Community Members (Britain, the Netherlands, France and Italy) was with the agreement of the remaining Community countries (and in a way they served as their representatives). Their participation was on a basis of either "all or none," and thus if Israel rejected one of them it would in fact be rejecting all the European Community countries.

Arab States used their influence to pressure against European participation in the MFO. Iraqi Foreign Minister, Saadon Hamadi, said on a visit in Rome that Iraq was ready to provide Italy with additional oil, but warned against Italy's participation in the Force.[24] Lebanon expressed concern over the possibility that the Community countries might participate in the Force. The Secretary to the Lebanese Foreign Minister summoned British Ambassador David Roberts and expressed concern over reports that Britain was considering sending troops to the Force.[25]

The US viewed the broadening of the list of participants -- especially the inclusion of leading Western powers -- as enhancing international recognition of the Israel-Egypt Peace Treaty. The change in the EC attitude was perceived by Israel as reflecting a more sympathetic sentiment on the part of the European countries towards Israel, particularly in the wake of the election of François Mitterand as President of France.[26] In Cairo Foreign Minister Kamal Hassan Ali welcomed the news that Australia, France and other Western countries were seriously considering contributing small units to the Force. He felt that this demonstrated the Free World's support of the peace process and its interest in the stability of the Middle East.[27]

There was a serious setback when British Foreign Minister Lord Carrington asserted (and French Foreign Minister Claude Cheysson had spoken in a similar vein) that the purpose of the MFO was to supervise Israel's withdrawal and, as Lord Carrington expressed it, "the return of Arab land to an Arab state." Lord Carrington, at the completion of a visit to Riyadh, reiterated that if the EC participated in the Force, "it would be on the basis of seeing the return of Arab territory to the Arabs and on no other basis at all."[28] In response to repeated statements by Lord Carrington that Britain's participation in the Force would not be on the basis of the Camp David Accords, but that Britain's purpose was to further the "principles of the Venice Declaration," Foreign Minister Yitzhak Shamir told the Knesset (Israel's Parliament) that Israel would "disqualify" from the Force any country which said it

was joining otherwise than "on the basis of ... Camp David."[29]
Prime Minister Begin stated that Israel would not agree to the
participation of States which would attach any additional documents
to the Peace Treaty documents.[30]   However, despite Carrington's
statements, Israeli officials were not prepared to say that Britain
was "disqualified" from participating.   They tried to avoid a
confrontation with Carrington.   A high Israeli official seemed to
imply that if the EC did not explicitly and directly link its
joining the Force to an anti-Camp David statement, Israel would not
activate its "disqualification" criterion.   Prime Minister Begin
warned the Europeans not to refer to the 1980 Venice Declaration,
since it was "a clear call for the PLO to be 'associated with' the
negotiations and for the establishment of a Palestinian
state."[31]

The Government of Israel, in a decision of November 8, 1981,
resolved that an absolute condition for European participation in
the Force was that neither the Venice Declaration nor the Saudi
peace plan be mentioned. Prime Minister Begin affirmed that:

1.   The purpose of the Force was not to supervise Israeli
     withdrawal from Sinai;
2.   There would not be any mention of the Venice Declaration;
3.   The only documents to serve as the basis for the Force were:
     a. the Camp David Accords and the Israel-Egypt Peace
        Treaty;
     b. President Carter's letter to President Sadat and Prime
        Minister Begin; and
     c. the MFO Protocol.[32]

Britain in an about-face agreed to contribute to the Force
without preconditions, and without basing the decision on the
Venice Declaration or the Saudi peace plan, but only on the Camp
David Accords. Prime Minister Thatcher stated that there was no
contradiction between the European position and the Camp David
Accords.[33] Israel requested that the Four accept the principles

of a US-Israeli joint statement issued, namely that the MFO is based on the Peace Treaty and that other Middle East policies advocated by the Europeans (i.e. the Venice Declaration) bear no relation to their proposed participation in the Force. The four countries consulted in order to draft a new statement in response.[34]

The US and the European countries agreed on a formula that would enable participation of the four European States in the MFO, following consultations in Washington between the Ambassadors of Great Britain, France, the Netherlands and Italy, and Secretary of State Alexander Haig. The formula was to be submitted for Israel's approval. The proposed declaration clearly upheld the Camp David Accords as the sole basis for establishing the Force which was to supervise the Israel-Egypt Peace Treaty and not Israel's withdrawal, as the Europeans requested. On the other hand, it included a very general statement wherein Europe reiterated its general commitment to the Venice Declaration.[35]

On November 12, 1981, the Four Europeans presented Prime Minister Begin with the compromise plan regarding their participation in the Force. The plan, which was approved by the other six EC members and the US, contained two clauses:

1.   The first referred to Camp David, the Peace Treaty, UN Security Council Resolution 242, and the agreement of Egypt, Israel and the US to constitute a Force.

2.   The second, which did not mention the planned Force, reiterated the support of the Four for the Venice Declaration.[36]

The Europeans, in an effort to balance their desire to strengthen Middle East stability since the murder of Egyptian President Anwar Sadat with their need to maintain good terms with the more radical Arab States and avoid antagonizing them, coupled their agreement to contribute to the MFO with statements reiterating Palestinian rights to self-determination, a phrase considered by Israel as a euphemism for the creation of a

Palestinian state. Israel's view was that the Europeans "will not bring the Venice Declaration through the back door. It is Camp David or nothing."[37]

On November 22, 1981, the four States consented to join the MFO on the basis of the agreement constituting the Force. This agreement states that it implements the Peace Treaty. The Treaty in turn states that it implements the Camp David Accord. Thus in the US view, Israel could consider that the Europeans were participating in the MFO on the basis of the Camp David Accord and were joining in its implementation. This could be regarded as a diplomatic victory for Israel, in that there was no mention of the Venice Declaration, or of the original British version according to which European participation was to have been described as part of the supervision over the withdrawal from Sinai.[38]

The first announcement explains the decision of the four participating States to send troops:

> The governments [of France, Italy, the Netherlands and the United Kingdom], after consulting their partners in the Ten, have decided, subject to their constitutional processes and to agreement on the practical and legal arrangements, to accede to the requests of the governments of Egypt, Israel and the U.S. to contribute to the MFO in Sinai. The four governments state that their participation in the MFO is based on the understanding that:
>
> 1.   The Force exists solely for the purpose of maintaining the peace in Sinai following Israeli withdrawal. It has no other role.
> 2.   The Force is being established in its present form in the absence of a UN decision on an international force, and its position will be reviewed should such a decision become possible.
> 3.   Participation by the four governments in the Force will not be taken either as committing them to or excluding them from participation in such other international peacekeeping arrangements as may have been or may be established in the region.
> 4.   Participation in the MFO by the four governments is without prejudice to their well-known policies on other aspects of the problems of the area.

In this statement the Four reserved their right to express

their policy-positions on the Middle East despite their decision to participate in the Force. Prime Minister Begin warned that he would not accept "new conditions" for participation in the MFO. The statement does not explicitly mention Camp David, but implicitly states that readiness to serve in the MFO entails acceptance of its mandate which is derived from the Peace Treaty. Israeli sources warned that if the "Venice Declaration" were specifically mentioned in the Community statement in connection with the members' participation in the MFO, such participation might be unacceptable to Begin.[39]

The supplementary statement of the Four, issued the next day, is worded as follows:

This decision is a symbol of our determination to achieve a comprehensive peace settlement following negotiations between the parties which would bring justice for all peoples and security for all the states of the area.

We welcomed the achievement of peace between Israel and Egypt as a first step towards this goal. Similarly we welcomed the Israeli withdrawal from Sinai as the first step towards the realization of the call for withdrawal contained in Resolution 242 of the UN Security Council which specifically declared inadmissible the acquisition of territory by war. And we believe that the international community has the duty to play its part, as necessary and with the agreement of the parties concerned, in peace arrangements in the Middle East.

We are ready to participate also in such arrangements in the other territories currently occupied in the context of Israeli withdrawal. We regard our support for the arrangements associated with the implementation of the Israeli-Egyptian peace treaty as quite distinct from and independent of the rest of the Camp David process.

In addition we wish to express our firm support for the Egyptian government and our belief in the need for stability and continuity in Egypt.

Our decision to participate in the MFO follows from the policy, as stated in the Declaration issued in Venice in June 1980 and in subsequent statements. This policy, while insisting on guarantees for the security of the State of Israel, places equal emphasis on justice for the Palestinian people and their right to self-determination. It also holds that the PLO must be involved in the process leading to a comprehensive peace.

We pledge ourselves to support the MFO. We also repeat that, together with our partners in the Ten, we will continue to work for the achievement of a comprehensive peace in the

Middle East in all ways consistent with the principles to which we hold.

Israel objected to the fact that the announcement of the Four was "couched in terms that indicate strong reservations concerning the very framework within which their accession to the MFO is to take place."[40] There was no mention in the announcement of acceptance of the Protocol under which the MFO was established, or of the Peace Treaty of which Israel felt the Protocol was an integral part. In fact, the Europeans stated that they regarded "support for the arrangements associated with the implementation of the Israeli-Egyptian Peace Treaty as quite distinct from and independent of the rest of the Camp David process." Moreover, Israel felt that the statement that "the force exists solely for the purpose of maintaining the peace in Sinai following Israeli withdrawal" and that "it has no other role" jeopardized the MFO's role in ensuring free navigation through the Strait of Tiran in accordance with Article 5 of the Peace Treaty.[41] Israel further objected to the fact that the supplementary statements of the Four contained "a highly selective reference to UN Resolution 242 which conveys the simplistic and erroneous impression that, under this resolution, Judea, Samaria, the Gaza district and the Golan Heights must be dealt with in precisely the same way as the Sinai was dealt with in the agreement with Egypt" (a process in which the EC countries indicated willingness to play a role). Israel's view was that the Four completely ignored the fact that these other areas constituted a totally different problem in several ways.

Thus in individual and joint statements the four European nations repeated longstanding doubts about the further utility of the Camp David peace process.[42] In the supplementary statement the Europeans called for, inter alia, self-determination for Palestinian Arabs -- a position which Israel interprets as supporting the creation of a Palestinian state and firmly opposes. The European statements stopped short of endorsing the Saudi Arabian peace proposal. That proposal, issued in August 1981, appeared to call for Arab recognition of Israel's right to exist, in return for Israel's withdrawal from lands it has occupied since the 1967 Middle East War. An Arab summit meeting in Fez, Morocco, at the end of November, broke up in disagreement over the Fahd plan.   Israel, which categorically rejected the Fahd plan, criticized the European statements and threatened to veto the European nations' participation because of their attitude toward Camp David and the question of Palestinian self-determination. The explicit reference to the Venice Declaration in the individual supplementary statements of the Four constituted, in Israel's view, a grave violation of the Camp David framework.   The latter advocates "self-determination" (i.e. another independent state) for the Palestinian Arabs, and "holds that the PLO must be involved in the process leading to a comprehensive peace."   According to Israel, this policy statement about the PLO ("in itself a prescription for chaos and war, rather than peace") was totally unrelated to the keeping of Egyptian-Israeli peace in the Sinai peninsula.[43]

The Community Statement, also issued on November 23, is as follows:

> The Ten consider that the decisions of France, Italy, the Netherlands and the United Kingdom to participate in the Multinational Force in Sinai meets the wish frequently expressed by the members of the Community to facilitate any progress in the direction of a comprehensive peace settlement in the Middle East on the basis of the mutual acceptance of the right to existence and security of all the States in the area and the need for the Palestinian people to exercise fully its right to self-determination.

This common declaration, on behalf of the ten members of the EC, including Greece, refers to the decision of the Four in such a way as to constitute approval, while the lack of clarity reflects the fact that Greece opposed the sending of troops. Greece was apparently responsible for the one-day delay in issuing the statement.   The Greek representative to the EC Summit in London refused to back a formula explicitly recognizing the validity of the Camp David Accords as the sole legal basis for the establishment of the Force.[44]

During the debate in the British House of Commons quite a few members found the statement "too complex and too hedged about with subordinate clauses." The British Secretary of State explained that it was difficult to get the words right when ten countries are involved. It was very important to get everybody to agree, "because since we want to work with all the parties in the Middle East, there is no point in trying to work with one party and not the other."[45]

The four countries' identical "national statements" to their parliaments asserted that their participation would "follow from" the Venice policy, and this negatively affected the atmosphere between them and Israel.[46] For example, the Dutch Foreign Minister, Max Van der Stoel, stated to the Dutch Parliament that EC participation in the Sinai Force did not mean renouncing the Venice Declaration.[47] The French Foreign Minister summarized the main points of the common position of the European Four, as embodied in the joint statement of the Four.[48]

Diplomatic consultations followed, and these, together with other documents not made public, may help to explain the discrepancies between the various European statements. Under strong pressure from the US, Israel agreed on December 3, 1981, to issue a Joint Israel-US declaration of principles on the MFO:[49]

> The United States and Israel note the decision of the United Kingdom, France, Italy and the Netherlands to contribute to the Multinational Force and Observers (MFO), to be established in accordance with the Treaty of Peace between Egypt and Israel.
> The United States and Israel reviewed the participation of these four countries in light of the following clarifications which they provided to the United States on November 26, 1981.
> -- That they recognize that the function of the MFO is as defined in the relevant Egyptian-Israeli agreements, and includes that of ensuring freedom of navigation through the Strait of Tiran in accordance with Article V of the Treaty of Peace; and
> -- That they have attached no political conditions, linked to Venice or otherwise, to their participation.
> The United States and Israel understand that the

34

participation of the four and any other participating
state is based upon the following:
-- The basis for participation in the MFO is the Treaty
of Peace between Egypt and Israel originated in the Camp
David Accords and the Protocol signed between Egypt and
Israel and witnessed by the U.S. on August 3, 1981 based
upon the letter from President Carter to President Sadat
and Prime Minister Begin of March 26, 1979.
-- All of the functions and responsibilities of the MFO
and of its constituent elements, including any
contingents that may be formed through European
participation, are defined in the Treaty of Peace and the
Protocol, and there can be no derogation or reservation
from any of them ...
     The United States understands and appreciates the
concerns expressed by the Government of Israel regarding
the statements made by the Four European contributors in
explaining their decision to participate in the MFO to
their own legislatures and publics. The United States
recognizes that some positions set forth in the
statements are at variance with its own positions with
respect to the future of the peace process as well as
with positions held by Israel as a Party to the Treaty of
Peace. The United States and Israel recognize that the
position held on any other aspects of the problems in the
area by any state which agrees to participate in the MFO
does not affect the obligation of that state to comply
fully with the terms of the Protocol which was negotiated
in accordance with the letter from President Carter to
President Sadat and Prime Minister Begin of March 26,
1979, and which is designed to help implement the Treaty
of Peace, which was concluded pursuant to the Camp David
Accords.
     The Treaty of Peace, in accordance with which the
MFO is established, represents the first step in a
process agreed on at Camp David whose ultimate goal is a
just, comprehensive, and durable settlement of the Middle
East conflict through the conclusion of peace treaties
based on Security Council resolutions 242 and 338. The
U.S. and Israel reiterate their commitment to the Camp
David Accords as the only viable and ongoing negotiating
process. They renew their determination to make early
meaningful progress in the autonomy talks.

Israel viewed this text as a balancing counter-weight to the
statements by the EC members, which reiterated the principles set
forth in the Venice Declaration advocating self-determination for
the Palestinians and recognizing the PLO as a vital factor in
reaching a settlement in the Middle East. Israel decided to insist
that the Four EC countries respond to the Israel-US declaration,

rather than to be satisfied with no reaction on their part. It asked the Four "to confirm their acceptance of the principles set forth" in the US-Israel statement. Lord Carrington in a letter to Secretary of State Alexander Haig stated that the declarations by the EC members did not include any conditions connected to the Venice Declaration or otherwise. On the other hand, he explained, the Statement of the Four set down that these States did not agree to any condition that would hinder the continuation of their wider policy in the Middle East.[50]

In fact, the European Four had actually previously accepted the key principles vital to Israel: that the Sinai Force is based on the Israel-Egypt Peace Treaty, and that the Europeans' own policy on the Middle East (the Venice Declaration) is not a condition to their participation in the Force. Likewise, when the four ambassadors presented their "Statement of the Four" at the Israel Foreign Ministry, each brought a letter from his minister to Foreign Minister Shamir, and at least two of these recognized that the Force would be based on the Peace Treaty. The letter from Italy's Emilio Colombo stated that the proposed participation was to be in support of the implementation of the relevant provisions of the Peace Treaty. Lord Carrington's letter was similar.[51]

Following intensive diplomatic efforts by the US, formulations acceptable to both sides were eventually agreed upon in January 1982. These formulations, based on the US-Israel declaration of December 1981, were agreed upon by the Four on January 13, 1982. Israel accepted the European offer at the end of January 1982.[52]

As anticipated, Arab reaction to European participation was negative. For example, a Syrian official handed a letter of protest to the French chargé d'affaires in response to the announcements of French Foreign Minister Claude Cheysson in Cairo regarding the MFO. It stated that the French position was detrimental to relations between France and Syria and the Arab world.[53] Faruq Qaddumi, head of the PLO political department, subsequently criticized Italy's decision to contribute units to the MFO, which he believed was merely a cover for US military encroachment.[54]

SIZE OF THE FORCE

The Peace Treaty does not define the size of the UN force to be stationed in the Sinai and in Zone D. The parties merely agreed to request the United Nations to provide forces and observers to supervise the implementation of the Protocol concerning Israeli withdrawal and security arrangements "and to employ their best efforts to prevent any violation of its terms."[55] This formulation was apparently a compromise between the parties, leaving the UN with the practical aspect of raising an appropriate force to effectively implement its task.[56] Israel had been interested in a large effective force, and Egypt in a smaller one. It was assumed that the UN force would be about 7000 strong, similar to UNEF-II.

During the negotiations on the MFO Protocol it became clear that some balance had to be found between the size of the force and its composition. It was obvious that the maintenance of a 7000-member force composed of troops from different countries and outside the overall supervision of the UN or another international organization would be unwieldy. Moreover, the heavy financial burden on Israel and Egypt would not have contributed to the stability of the force.

According to the compromise reached in the Protocol, the MFO shall consist of a headquarters, three infantry battalions totalling not more than 2000 troops, a coastal patrol unit and an observer unit, an aviation element and logistics and signal units.[57] The Force's three infantry battalions, as required, total not more than 2000 troops. The civilian observer unit, as well as the various military support units, employ approximately another 600 military and 800 civilian personnel of Egyptian and other nationalities.[58] There are some women in the MFO in those units that ordinarily employ them.

LEGAL BASIS FOR PARTICIPATION

The Director-General of the MFO entered into negotiations

with each of the contributing States in order to give legal expression to their participation in the Force in the form of a written text. It was necessary in a separate agreement with each State to specify its exact contribution in terms of personnel and equipment. The procedure leading to the agreement with France, which was followed mutatis mutandis for other States, was as follows: France was concerned in principle over negotiations between herself as a State, on one side, and the Director-General as a private person devoid of the status of international agent, on the other.

In effect, France was asking the Director-General to produce written evidence of his legal status and capacity to enter into agreements. M. Couve de Murville noted the novelty of the procedure before the French National Assembly. He pointed out that this was not the usual situation of approving an agreement with one or more foreign governments or with a recognized international organization. In the case of the MFO, there was an exchange of letters between the French Foreign Minister and a US citizen nominated by the Egyptian and Israeli Governments, without the US being mentioned.[59]

Since France questioned the Director-General's judicial capacity to negotiate and conclude a treaty, she requested that the parties issue Mr. Hunt a "letter of habilitation." France was satisfied with Egyptian and Israeli letters thus empowering the Director-General.[60]

The final agreement with France consists of two Exchanges of Letters between the French Foreign Minister and the MFO Director-General.[61] This was submitted to, and approved by, the French Parliament.[62]

The document containing the terms of the agreement on Australia's participation in the MFO are likewise in the form of two Exchanges of Letters constituting the agreement between the MFO Director-General and the Australian Foreign Minister, Tony Street. The agreement gives details of the overall size and shape of the Australian contingent and the terms on which it will participate in the Force. An Aide-Mémoire is also attached to the first letter from the Director-General. This document, which does not hold treaty status, gives guidelines to governments preparing to assign troops for service with the MFO.[63]

According to Australia's Foreign Minister, the above agreement and related MFO Protocol, which establish the basis for the Australian participation and protect the status of Australian personnel in the Force, "are binding in international law on Egypt and Israel as well as the MFO."[64] On the basis of this statement, at least, Australia did not seem to question the legal personality of the MFO or the treaty-making capacity of its Director-General. It is unclear through what legal mechanism Australia considered the agreement between itself and the MFO to be binding upon Egypt and Israel.

According to Professor Ruth Lapidoth, the scope of the term "international organization" is very wide and would seem to include the MFO. In support of this view she cites various documents in which the MFO is referred to as an "international organization."[65] If this is the case, guidance may be sought in the draft articles on the law of treaties between States and international organizations or between international organizations. In accordance with the latter, an "international organization" means an "intergovernmental organization."[66] According to the Commentary of the International Law Commission, no attempt was made to prejudge the amount of legal capacity that an entity requires in order to be considered an international organization within the meaning of the draft articles. They are intended to apply to treaties to which one or more international organizations are parties, irrespective of the status of the organizations involved and regardless of their purpose or character. The draft articles are applicable to any international organization that has the capacity to conclude at least one treaty.[67] Clearly the MFO has fulfilled this criterion, having concluded agreements with the contributing States.

The draft articles regulate treaties providing for obligations or rights for third States. An obligation arises for a third State from a provision of a treaty if the parties to the treaty intend the provision to be the means of establishing the obligation and the third State expressly accepts the obligation in writing.[68] Although Egypt and Israel are not commonly thought of as "third parties" in terms of the MFO and the contributing States, this may indeed be their status in this context. As an example of a duty of a party mentioned in the MFO-contributing State treaties, one may single out financial obligations whereby the MFO undertakes to reimburse the contributing States. Indirectly this affects Egypt and Israel -- as well as the US, in that they provide the funds to finance such reimbursements. However, the obligation upon them stems from different instruments. For example, Egypt and Israel undertake in the MFO Protocol that the expenses of the MFO which are not covered by other sources shall be borne equally by the parties (Article 7). Any financial obligation incurred by the MFO as an expense in relation to a contributing State is a separate legal undertaking. At the same time, Article 7 of the Protocol perhaps may be considered as written acceptance of any financial obligation the MFO undertakes towards contributing States, upon which the parties have agreed.

COMPOSITION AND CONTRIBUTIONS

The ten-nation peacekeeping force was constituted of contingents from the US, Australia, New Zealand, Colombia, Fiji, Uruguay, the United Kingdom, the Netherlands, Italy and France.

The contributing States have agreements with the MFO for their contingents to remain from two to five years.[69] (Initially Colombia, Fiji and Uruguay signed up for five years, and six other participants for a two-year term.) The US is committed to keep its troops for the duration of the MFO.[70] All agreements were subject to renewal, the shortest in the Spring of 1984.

Table 1 summarizes the nature of the personnel contributed by each country. This is followed by a description of the contingent of each participant.[71]

Table 1.   M U L T I N A T I O N A L   F O R C E   A N D   O B S E R V E R S

CONTRIBUTIONS OF PARTICIPATING COUNTRIES

COUNTRY	CONTINGENT	PERSONNEL
1. Australia	A portion of the Helicopter Section of the MFO Aviation Support Group including eight (8) UH-1H helicopters.	Approximately 109 personnel including a Headquarters Staff, Air Crewmen, Air Traffic Control Sections; Maintenance Section, Airfield Services personnel and officers for the Force Commander's staff.
2. Colombia	An Infantry Battalion consisting of three (3) Rifle Companies, and a Headquarter's Company.	Approximately 500 men (all ranks) plus officers for the Force Commander's staff.
3. Fiji	An Infantry Battalion consisting of three (3) Rifle Companies, and a Headquarter's Company.	Approximately 500 men (all ranks) plus officers for the Force Commander's staff.
4. France	The Fixed-wing element of the Aviation Support Group consisting of one (1) Transall C160, and two (2) Twin Otters.	A maximum of 42 personnel including a Contingent Command Section, aircraft crews, maintenance personnel, loading supervisors, and officers for the Force Commander's staff.
5. Italy	A Naval Contingent consisting of three (3) Minesweepers and maintenance-related equipment.	A maximum of 90 Naval personnel including a Command Section, ship complements, maintenance personnel, and officers for the Force Commander's staff.

6. The Netherlands	A Military Signals Unit and a Military Police Unit.	The Military Signals Unit of a maximum of 81 personnel includes a Company Headquarters, Company Support, MFO Force Headquarters, Signal Staff section, and a Platoon North and Platoon South including Platoon Headquarters and support personnel. The Military Police Unit of a maximum of 21 personnel includes a Provost Marshal Element and a Criminal Investigation Element and a military police detachment, and officers for the Force Commander's staff.
7. New Zealand	A portion of the Helicopter Section of the MFO Aviation Support Group including two (2) UH-1H helicopters.	Approximately 35 personnel including a Helicopter Section, and airfield services section, and officers for the Force Commander's staff.
8. United Kingdom	A Headquarters Company for administrative and security functions.	A maximum of 35 personnel including Camp Commandant, Administrative Section, Quartermaster Section, Camp Security Section, Transportation Section and officers for the Force Commander's staff.
9. United States	An Infantry Battalion Task Force consisting of an Infantry Battalion Headquarters and its associated Headquarters Company, three (3) Rifle Companies, a Combat Support Company, a Helicopter Support Element, a Signal Support Element.	Approximately 800 personnel.

M U L T I N A T I O N A L   F O R C E   A N D   O B S E R V E R S   (cont.)

CONTRIBUTIONS OF PARTICIPATING COUNTRIES

COUNTRY	CONTINGENT	PERSONNEL
United states	Logistics Support Element	Approximately 350 personnel
	Civilian Observers	Approximately 25 civilian observers and support personnel, and officers for the Force Commander's staff.
10. Uruguay	A Transportation Company	Approximately 70 personnel (all ranks) including a Command Section, Operations Section, Dispatch Section Light Vehicle Platoon, a Heavy Vehicle Platoon; officers for the Force Commander's staff, and since March 1983, 35 Road Engineers.

Australia and New Zealand

Australia and New Zealand are contributing a helicopter unit, including about 130 people and 10 helicopters as the rotary wing air unit for the Force. The Australian contingent, with its eight UH-1H helicopters, has joined with the New Zealand contingent to form the MFO's ANZAC Rotary Wing Aviation Unit.[72] New Zealand provides 35 men and two helicopters to the ANZAC helicopter unit.

Unit helicopters provide primary transportation for the MFO observers in their verification missions throughout the four treaty Zones. They are also used for logistic support flights to remote outposts in the sectors assigned to the Colombian and Fijian battalions. They transport patrols to and from temporary positions and mobile night positions, and are on 24-hour call for medical evacuation. The ANZAC unit also provides airfield, flight control and meteorological services to all MFO aviation elements. Both Australian and New Zealand pilots have undertaken numerous rescue and medical evacuation flights, many of which involved the civilian residents of the area. In forming themselves into a joint ANZAC unit, the Australians and New Zealanders have continued a tradition that began during the First World War when troops from both countries served jointly in the Mediterranean region.

Colombia

The 500-strong Colombian Battalion is headquartered at El Gorah in the North and is assigned the observation posts and checkpoints in Zone C (see map). The Colombian infantry men also conduct reconnaissance patrols in the same sectors. Called Colombia tres in reference to the fact that the battalion is Colombia's third contribution to international peacekeeping, the contingent has distinguished itself by a disciplined approach to the manning of observation posts, and dedication to base improvement projects.

Fiji

Fiji is also contributing an infantry battalion (about 500 soldiers). The Fiji Battalion conducts patrols and mans observation posts and checkpoints in the northern and most populated sectors of Zone C. Based at El Gorah, the battalion also provides technical engineering assistance in road building and repair. Fiji is one of the world's most consistent contributors to international peacekeeping and has therefore been able to field an MFO contingent with considerable experience. Over half of the Fijian soldiers in the MFO battalion had served in the Fijian contingent in UNIFIL, the UN peacekeeping operation in South Lebanon, and therefore provided a valuable reserve of practical knowledge during the early days in the Sinai. (Although other contingents serve six months in the desert on a rotation basis, the Fijians remain an entire year which also contributes to their considerable professionalism.)

France

France is contributing a fixed wing unit of three airplanes and their crews, which number about 40 people. With one C-160 Transall aircraft and two DH-6 Twin Otters, the French contingent provides the MFO's air links between its two main bases as well as Cairo and Tel Aviv. Its duties include the transport of supplies, equipment and personnel, and official visitors. The functions are strictly defined in the agreement between France and the MFO, according to which "These functions may only be changed with the mutual agreement of the Government of the French Republic and the Director-General of the MFO."[73]

Italy

Italy provides a naval contingent of about 90 officers and sailors, as well as minesweepers.[74] Four ships are used on a rotation basis to keep three on station with the MFO, while the fourth undergoes maintenance in Italy. They sail the southern third of the Gulf of Aqaba between the Dahab parallel and Ras Muhammed, a 60-nautical mile area. They are responsible for monitoring the Treaty provision ensuring freedom of navigation through the Strait of Tiran, the very tight area off Sharm-El-Sheikh, at the southern entrance to the Gulf of Aqaba. The contingent is headquartered at the Egyptian port of Sharm-El-Sheikh. When not aboard ship the sailors use living and eating facilities at the MFO's South Base. Working closely with MFO observation posts in the southern sector of Zone C, the Italian vessels average more than twelve hours per day on patrol during both daylight and night-time hours.

The Netherlands

The Netherlands contingent is divided into two units:

The Military Signals Unit mans and maintains the communications system between the El Gorah headquarters and all MFO units in the Sinai, which includes the remote communications relay sites throughout the Colombian, Fijian and US Battalion sectors. The 81 Dutch communicators are experts in the equipment they operate and fluent in English, the MFO's official operating language.

The Military Police Unit includes a Provost Marshall Element, a Criminal Investigation Element and a Military Police Detachment. It consists of 21 persons.[75]

Norway

Norway, although not a participating State in the sense of contributing a contingent, has provided the Force Commander and the support of three experienced officers for duty with the Force Commander's staff.

United Kingdom

Britain contributes a Headquarters Company of about 35 officers and men. The Company provides administrative, clerical and logistic support to the Force Commander's staff.

The United States

About half the MFO is manned by the US. According to Public Law 97-132, the number of members of the US Armed Forces assigned or detailed by the US Government to the MFO may not exceed 1200 at any one time (Sec. 3 (a)(4)). The US provides an infantry battalion, a logistics support unit and a civilian observer unit.

The Infantry Battalion consists of 800 soldiers and mans the observation posts and checkpoints in the two southern sectors of Zone C, which include the islands of Tiran and Sanafir in the Strait of Tiran. Housed and headquartered at the MFO's South Base, the battalion also conducts reconnaissance patrols and provides its own helicopter and motor transport. The first American unit to participate was a battalion from the 82nd Airborne Division, which was replaced after six months by a battalion from the 101st Airborne Division. They serve on a rotating half-year basis.

The Logistics Support Unit, although based at El Gorah, manages the MFO supply system, provides the entire Force with fully-staffed medical dispensaries at both the North and South Bases, performs weapons and equipment maintenance, as well as explosive ordnance disposal.

The Civilian Observer Unit consists of up to fifty civilians, half of whom have been seconded from the US Government's Foreign Service and half recruited from the private sector for their expertise in military matters, namely former members of the Armed Services with service experience. The unit conducts verification missions throughout the four Zones.[76]

Uruguay

The Uruguayan contingent originally consisted of a 75-man transportation unit to operate the MFO's truck fleet. In March 1983, Uruguay, at the request of the MFO, replaced 35 of its motor transport personnel with engineering specialists whose task it is to maintain the MFO's vital road network.

ALTERNATIVES

At the time the MFO was constituted, Canada announced that she would not send soldiers to the MFO, since a sufficient number of other countries agreed to participate in the Force. Her Foreign Minister did not rule out the possibility that Canada might participate, but since at the time the European Four agreed to send contingents, this was unnecessary.[77] The MFO considered that there were States capable of committing themselves to support the Force, but no discussions or arrangements were taking place until it became certain that one of the current participants would be unable to continue.[78] Both parties to the Peace Treaty were satisfied with the composition of the MFO and preferred a continuation of the status quo to a search for new participants.[79]

The Australian, Dutch, British, French, Italian and New Zealand contingents were due to terminate their service in the MFO in April 1984. On August 5, 1983, the MFO officially extended an invitation to these countries to renew their agreements of participation. Both Egypt and Israel in February 1984 requested that these contingents extend their participation.

Australia, where in March 1983 the left-wing Labor Party (ALP) defeated the ruling Liberal-National Party that had formed the Government since 1975, agreed to remain for an additional period of two years, until April 1986, when it will withdraw its contingent. It may be assumed that this is due to domestic problems, and to its negative attitude towards the US that is manifested through its policy regarding the MFO.[80]

It was expected that New Zealand would withdraw as well, since the new left-oriented government that took over in 1984 was critical of certain aspects of US foreign policy. In March 1985, however, New Zealand announced that it was interested in remaining in the MFO and would look into the possibility of doing so. Since the New Zealand contingent formed part of the integrated ANZAC unit within the MFO, it was necessary to look at the implications of Australia's decision for New Zealand. It would not be easy, for logistic reasons, to come up with alternatives, but New Zealand was anxious to demonstrate its wish to seek peace in the Middle East. As pointed out by Professor Alan James, "In this manner the Government both distinguished itself from Australia (always a consideration for a lesser neighbour) and engaged in a bit of fence-mending with the United States."[81]

In view of Australia's forthcoming withdrawal, Israeli Foreign Minister Shamir in March 1985 officially asked Canada to participate in the MFO. Egypt had made a similar request earlier. In April 1985 Canada announced that in response to requests from the Governments of Egypt and Israel, and subject to the successful negotiation of an agreement which adequately meets Canadian essential interests, the Canadian Government decided in principle to participate in the MFO. The last time Canada joined a non-UN international force was as part of the four-country observer group (the International Commission of Control and Supervision) sent to Vietnam in 1973 after the Paris peace accords as a monitoring force and withdrawn a year later. Since then, Canada refused involvement in any treaty-supervision mission organized outside the UN. Participation in the MFO therefore would seem to represent a policy change toward international peacekeeping duties.[82]

In terms of technical and specialized manpower requirements, a developing country was not suitable for replacing Australia. It was necessary to secure the participation of a State possessing the equipment and capable of fulfilling the technical tasks performed by Australia. Canada would be sending about 100 troops and a number of helicopters (probably in the order of eight) to assume Australia's role, "without any diminution thereof."

In the event that no suitable alternative contributor could be found, it was assumed by the MFO that it would contract the required aircraft and recruit two other States to contribute contingents.

NOTES

(1) Peace Treaty, Annex I, Art. 6, para. 8.
(2) See Ahmad Shahin, "The Multinational Peacekeeping Force in Sinai," Shu'un Filastiniyyah (No. 117), Aug. 1981, pp. 195-99 (Arabic).
(3) MFO Protocol, Art. 4.
(4) Identical US letters to Egypt and Israel, Aug. 3, 1981, 20 Int'l Legal Materials (No. 5) 1190 (Sept. 1981).
(5) MFO Annex, Art. 3.
(6) Alfred Pijpers, "European Participation in the Sinai Peace-keeping Force (MFO)," in European Foreign Policy-Making and the Arab-Israeli Conflict 211-23 (David Allen and Alfred Pijpers eds. The Hague 1984) (hereinafter: Pijpers).
(7) Nathan A. Pelcovits, Peacekeeping on Arab-Israeli Fronts: Lessons from the Sinai and Lebanon 84-85, 79 (Boulder 1984).
(8) P.L. 97-132, Sec. 5(c). 3 U.S. Code Congressional and Administrative News, 97th Congress, 1st Sess. 2742-43, 2745 (1981).
(9) MFO Annual Report, 1983, p. 10.
(10) Identical letters from Haig to Egypt and Israel, Aug. 3, 1981, paras. 1, 3A, supra note 4.
(11) Jerusalem Post, Oct. 23, 1981, p. 1, col. 5.
(12) See MFO Annex, Art. 6. MFO Annual Report, 1983, pp. 10-11.
(13) Pijpers, p. 213. For the attitudes of the individual EC members, see Pijpers, pp. 216 ff.
(14) Haaretz (Israeli daily newspaper, Hebrew), Jan. 5, 1982. For French policy, see Pijpers, pp. 216-17.
(15) See 52 Australian Foreign Affairs Record (No. 11) 573 ff. (Nov. 1981). Jerusalem Post, Oct. 23, 1981, p. 2, col. 7. See statement by Tony Street, Minister for Foreign Affairs to House of Representatives on May 26, 1981, 52 Australian Foreign Affairs Record (No. 5) 263-69 (May 1981). Robert O'Neill, "The Sinai Commitment: Dangers, Responsibilities and Opportunities," 52 ibid. (No. 11) 550-52 (Nov. 1981). For the debate in Parliament over participation see Australia, Representatives, Oct. 22, 1981, pp. 2412-47.

On November 24, 1981, Prime Minister Fraser stated that the announcement of the Four to participate met the Commonwealth Government's requirement for a balanced multinational force and made possible Australia's participation. On January 1, 1982,

Fraser announced that with Egypt's and Israel's acceptance of participation of the "Four," the MFO "achieved the degree of balance which will enable Australia to participate in this peace-keeping initiative." See also 53 Australian Foreign Affairs Record (No. 2) 84, 91 (Feb. 1982). Shlomo Shafir, Davar (Israeli daily, Hebrew), Feb. 2, 1982.

(16) TV Interview, Nov. 15, 1981, cited in Hazofe (Israeli daily, Hebrew), Nov. 17, 1981, p. 1; Haaretz, Nov. 17, 1981.

(17) Hazofe, Oct. 28, 1981, p. 2.

(18) Washington Post, Oct. 22, 1981, cited in Jerusalem Post, Oct. 23, 1981, p. 2. See Pijpers, pp. 217-18.

(19) Hazofe, Oct. 23, 1981, p. 1. See Pijpers, pp. 219-20.

(20) Corriere della Sera, Oct. 30, 1981; cited in Pijpers, p. 218.

(21) See Pijpers, p. 219.

(22) Hulda Liberanoma, "Israel and the MFO," Haaretz, Nov. 16, 1981, p. 10. See Corriere della Sera, Nov. 10, 11, 1981.

(23) Text of the Declaration, June 12-13, 1980, in Laurent Lucchini, "La Force Internationale du Sinai: Le Maintien de la Paix Sans l'O.N.U.," 29 Annuaire Français de Droit International 121, at 132 (1983) (hereinafter: Lucchini).

(24) Hazofe, Oct. 22, 1981, p. 1. See Pijpers, p. 214.

(25) Hazofe, Oct. 28, 1981, p. 2.

(26) Jerusalem Post, Oct. 10, 1981, p. 1, col. 5.

(27) Hazofe, Oct. 23, 1981, p. 1.

(28) Jerusalem Post Nov. 6, 1981, p. 18.

(29) Ibid.

(30) Haaretz, Nov. 6, 1981, p. 1.

(31) David Landau, Jerusalem Post, Nov. 6, 1981, p. 1.

(32) Haaretz, Nov. 9, 1981, p. 1; Hazofe, Nov. 9, 1981, p. 1.

(33) Hazofe, Nov. 10, 1981, p. 1.

(34) Jerusalem Post, Nov. 12, 1981.

(35) Haaretz, Nov. 11, 1981, p. 2.

(36) Haaretz, Nov. 13, 1981, p. 1.

(37) N.Y. Times, "News of the Week in Review," Nov. 29, 1981, p. 2 1E.

(38) Haaretz, Nov. 17, 1981.

(39) Jerusalem Post, Nov. 23, 1981, p. 1.

(40) Israel Information Centre. Information Briefing 426/29.11.81/4.06.0814.

(41) Art. 6, para, 2(d) of Annex I of the Peace Treaty refers to a function of UN forces of "Ensuring the freedom of navigation through the Strait of Tiran in accordance with Article V of the Treaty of Peace." Art. 5, para. 2 of the Peace Treaty mentions freedom of navigation and overflight through the Strait of Tiran as well as the Gulf of Aqaba. Egypt was apparently interested in reducing the scope of freedom of navigation, while Israel tried to include the Gulf of Aqaba in Annex I. In any case, there is a discrepancy between these two provisions.

(42) 39 Congressional Quarterly, Weekly Report (No. 41) 1935 ff., at 1940 (Oct. 10, 1981). For the French statement see

Lucchini, pp. 133-34 and n. 43 for French policy.

(43) Ibid.

(44) Haaretz, Nov. 22, 1981, p. 1. Pijpers, pp. 220, 221.

(45) Interview with Gordon Martin for BBC World Service, London Press Service, Verbatim Service 186/81, Nov. 23, 1981, p. 1.

(46) Jerusalem Post, Dec. 4, 1981, p. 1.

(47) Haaretz, Dec. 6, 1981, p. 1. For the British supplementary statement, cited above, see London Press Service, Verbatim Service 185/81, Nov. 23, 1981, pp. 1-2.

(48) France. Journal Officiel Assemblée Nationale, Questions et Réponses. Jan. 25, 1982, p. 319; cited in Lucchini, p. 134, n. 43.

(49) Jerusalem Post, Dec. 4, 1981, p. 4; see Pijpers, p. 215

(50) Haaretz, Dec. 4, 1981, p. 1. See interview with British Ambassador to Cairo. 'Abd-al-Nabi, Hadayat. Al Siyasah al Duwaliyyah (No. 67), Jan. 1982, pp. 151-54 (Arabic).

(51) Pijpers, p. 215 and n. 25.

(52) Ibid., p. 216. 29 Keesing's Contemporary Archives 31907A (1983).

(53) Haaretz, Jan. 5, 1982.

(54) 3 Al Fajr (No. 100) 6 (April 2, 1982). See however, Daily Telegraph, Feb. 26, 1982, p. 6, for Oman's positive reaction.

(55) Peace Treaty, Annex I, Art. 6, para. 1.

(56) "The Multinational Force" (Hebrew), Ma'arachot (No. 283), at 28 (July 1982).

(57) MFO Annex, Art. 19. A 2500-member force "was more or less a straight compromise between Israel's wish for about 5000 troops and Egypt's disinclination to have any at all." Alan James, "Symbol in Sinai: The Multinational Force and Observers" (mimeo) 6 (July 11, 1984) (hereinafter: James).

(58) MFO "Background and Mission" (mimeo) 4 (Rome, Nov. 17, 1982). See Pelcovits, p. 73.

(59) France. Journal Officiel, Assemblée Nationale, Débats, April 22, 1982, p. 1257; cited in Lucchini, p. 135, n. 46.

(60) Lucchini, p. 135.

(61) France. Journal Officiel, May 7, 1982, p. 1292; cited in Lucchini, p. 135 and n. 47.

(62) Law No. 82-376, May 6, 1982. France. Journal Officiel 1982, p. 1292; cited in Lucchini, p. 136 and n. 50.

(63) Texts in 53 Australian Foreign Affairs Record (No. 3) 134-37 (March 1982).

(64) Ibid., p. 133.

(65) Lapidoth, p. 387 and n. 44. On the legal personality of the MFO, see ibid., pp. 384-87.

(66) [1982-2(II)] Y.B. Int'l L. Comm'n 17, at 18, Art. 1(i) (E/CN.4/SER.A/1982/Add.1 (Part 2)).

The UN General Assembly, at its 39th Session, decided that a UN Conference on this subject will be held in Vienna from February 18 to March 21, 1986. The draft articles are referred to the Conference as the basic proposal for its consideration (99th Plen.

Mtg., Dec. 13, 1984). See A/RES/39/86, Jan. 18, 1985.

(67) ILC Commentary, ibid., p. 20, paras. 21, 22, 23.

(68) Art. 35, ibid., p. 42.

(69) The four European countries, Australia and New Zealand agreed to serve for two years; Fiji, Colombia and Uruguay for five years. Transcript of Press Conference by MFO Director-General, Mr. Hunt, with Rome Representatives of International Wire Services, Rome, January 17, 1983 (hereinafter: Hunt Press Conference, Jan. 17, 1983), p. 6.

(70) MFO House Hearings, pp. 58-60.

(71) MFO, "Background and Mission," Rome, Nov. 17, 1982, pp. 7-9. Unless otherwise indicated, the information below is from MFO Annual Report, 1983, pp. 15-19.

(72) In the port of Sidney there was initially a strike against sending Australian soldiers to Sinai. See 53 Australian Foreign Affairs Record (No. 3) 133, 135 (March 1982). See 53 ibid. (No. 6) 399 (June 1982) for a visit by Australian Defense Minister.

(73) Cited in Lucchini, p. 135.

(74) MFO Annual Report, 1984, p. 16. The first of the three Italian mine sweepers ("Palma") destined for the MFO left La Spezia harbor after a formal ceremony. Its voyage was suddenly interrupted while it was still in Italian coastal waters and anchored in Messina, Sicily. Sources at the Italian Ministry of Defense said that the stop was routine. Parliamentary sources stated that the Italian Government's decision to participate in the MFO was not formally approved by the Parliament. Thus the status of the ship was like that of a citizen wishing to leave a country without a valid passport. The question was raised by the Communists, who accused the Government that the decision was "without law or international agreement." After the ship set out, the Communist Party demanded a joint meeting of the foreign affairs committee and the parliamentary committee in order to hear additional details from the Defense and Foreign Ministers before voting on the formal approval of the mission. Politically there was no fear of the Communist Party's causing problems to the coalition Government led by Giovanni Spadolini, as it supported Italian participation in the MFO. (Ma'ariv (Israeli daily, Hebrew), March 15, 1982, p. 7.)

(75) The Netherlands Government on February 15, 1982, officially approved the participation of a Dutch unit in the MFO. On February 1, 75 men of the signal corps and six officers and NCOs began their special training. All major political parties approved the Government's decision and therefore Parliamentary approval was easily achieved.

(76) See Major Cornelis Homan, "MFO: Peacekeeping in the Middle East," 63 Military Rev. (No. 9) 2, at 5,7. (Sept. 1983). On the arrival of the US contingent see Newsweek, March 29, 1982, p. 27; Yedi'ot Aharonot (Israeli daily, Hebrew) Feb. 28, 1982. On the attitudes of the US contingents generally, see David R. Segal et al., "Paratroopers as Peacekeepers: U.S. Participation in the Sinai Constabulary Mission," Paper presented at 78th Mtg., American Sociological Association, Aug. 31, 1983.

(77) Haaretz, Nov. 22, 1981, p. 1; Nov. 25, 1981, p. 2.

(78) Hunt Press Connference, Jan. 17, 1983, p. 10.

(79) Hirsh Goodman, Jerusalem Post, Feb. 3, 1984, p. 1, (also Int'l Ed., Feb. 5-11, 1984, p. 4). MFO Annual Report, 1984 p. 29

(80) On Australian opposition to participation in the MFO, see Australia, Representatives, May 7, 1984, pp. 1917, 1918, statement by Mr. Hayden, Minister for Foreign Affairs. On the attitude of the Labor Party, see Representatives, Oct. 22, 1981, pp. 2417 ff.

(81) Alan James, "Symbol in Sinai: The Multinational Force and Observers," 14 Millenium (No. 3) (Dec. 1985). Press statement of David Lange, Prime Minister of New Zealand, March 14, 1985.

(82) See generally Geoffrey A. H. Pearson, "Canadian Attitudes to Peacekeeping," in Peacekeeping: Appraisals and Proposals 118-29 (Henry Wiseman ed. N.Y. 1983) and Rod B. Byers, "Peacekeeping and Canadian Defense Policy: Ambivalence and Uncertainty," ibid., pp. 130-56. At one point, Egypt was opposed to Canadian participation, since it is too close to the US. Canada, Office of the Prime Minister, [Press] Release, "Canada to Join Sinai Peacekeeping Force," April 11, 1985. "Canada to Take Sinai Peninsula Peacekeeper Role, " London Free Press, April 13, 1985.

4
Functions

The MFO Protocol stipulates that the mission of the Force is to undertake the functions and responsibilities outlined in the Peace Treaty for the United Nations Forces and Observers.[1] These responsibilities relate to the security arrangements provided by the Treaty.

A. TEMPORARY FUNCTIONS

The role of the UN in the withdrawal of Israeli forces from the Sinai is described in the Peace Treaty, which provides:

United Nations Forces

1. The Parties shall request that United Nations forces be deployed as necessary to perform the functions described in this Appendix up to the time of completion of final Israeli withdrawal. For that purpose, the Parties agree to the redeployment of the United Nations Emergency Force.

2. United Nations forces will supervise the implementation of this Appendix and will employ their best efforts to prevent any violation of its terms.

3. When United Nations forces deploy in accordance with the provisions of Articles I and II of this Appendix, they will perform the functions of verification in limited force zones in accordance with Article VI of Annex I, and will establish check points, reconnaissance patrols, and observation posts in the temporary buffer zones described in Article II above. Other functions of the United Nations forces which concern the interim buffer zone are described in Article V of this Appendix.[2]

The parties envisaged that UNEF-II would continue to function throughout the withdrawal period. As Israeli armed forces withdrew at each phase, UN forces were immediately to enter the evacuated areas to establish interim and temporary buffer zones, "for the purpose of maintaining a separation of forces." The deployment of UN forces was to precede the movement of any other personnel into these areas.[3]

UN forces were to escort Israeli convoys evacuating forces and equipment until the completion of the interim withdrawal.[4] The United Nations Forces and Observers were to report any violations to the Joint Commission.[5] The implementation of these functions, in the absence of an acceptable multinational force at the time of Israel's withdrawal, was described above in Chapter 1.

B. PERMANENT FUNCTIONS

The long-term general functions of the MFO are to supervise the implementation of the Peace Treaty and to prevent violations of its provisions, including

(1) to ensure the freedom of navigation through the Strait of Tiran;[6] and

(2) to oversee the limitation of forces and armaments. The Treaty determines the final lines and zones in the Sinai and the degree of armaments therein, as follows:[7]

a. Zone A [near the Suez Canal; see map]

    (1) Zone A is bounded on the east by line A (red line) and on the west by the Suez Canal and the east coast of the Gulf of Suez, as shown on Map 1.

    (2) An Egyptian armed force of one mechanized infantry division and its military installations, and field fortifications, will be in this Zone.

    (3) The main elements of that division will consist of:

        (a) Three mechanized infantry brigades.

        (b) One armored brigade.

    (c)   Seven field artillery battalions including up to 126 artillery pieces.

    (d)   Seven anti-aircraft artillery battalions including individual surface-to-air missiles and up to 126 anti-aircraft guns of 37 mm and above.

    (e)   Up to 230 tanks.

    (f)   Up to 480 armored personnel vehicles of all types.

    (g)   Up to a total of twenty-two thousand personnel.

b.   Zone B

    (1)   Zone B is bounded by line B (green line) on the east and by line A (red line) on the west, as shown on Map 1.

    (2)   Egyptian border units of four battalions equipped with light weapons and wheeled vehicles will provide security and supplement the civil police in maintaining order in Zone B. The main elements of the four border battalions will consist of up to a total of four thousand personnel.

    (3)   Land based, short range, low power, coastal warning points of the border patrol units may be established on the coast of this Zone.

    (4)   There will be in Zone B field fortifications and military installations for the four border battalions.

c.   Zone C [subject to maximal limitations]

    (1)   Zone C is bounded by line B (green line) on the west and the international boundary and the Gulf of Aqaba on the east, as shown on Map 1.

    (2)   Only United Nations [amended by the Protocol to: MFO] forces and Egyptian civil police will be stationed in Zone C.

    (3)   The Egyptian civil police armed with light weapons will perform normal police functions within this Zone.

    (4)   The United Nations Force will be deployed within Zone C

and perform its functions as defined in Article VI of this Annex.

(5) The United Nations Force will be stationed mainly in camps located within the following stationing areas shown on Map 1, and will establish its precise locations after consultations with Egypt:

    (a) In that part of the area in the Sinai lying within about 20 km. of the Mediterranean Sea and adjacent to the international boundary.

    (b) In the Sharm el Sheikh area.

d.   Zone D [East of the international border]

(1) Zone D is bounded by line D (blue line) on the east and the international boundary on the west, as shown on Map 1.

(2) In this Zone there will be an Israeli limited force of four infantry battalions, their military installations, and field fortifications, and United Nations observers.

(3) The Israeli forces in Zone D will not include tanks, artillery and anti-aircraft missiles except individual surface-to-air missiles.

(4) The main elements of the four Israeli infantry battalions will consist of up to 180 armored personnel vehicles of all types and up to a total of four thousand personnel.

Access across the international boundary is permitted through entry checkpoints designated by each party and under its control. Such access shall be in accordance with laws and regulations of each country. Only those field fortifications, military installations, forces, and weapons specifically permitted by Annex I of the Peace Treaty shall be in the Zones.

In addition to overseeing the ground regime, the MFO is responsible for supervising the aerial and naval military regimes in these Zones. The MFO is to supervise the implementation of these provisions on the limitation of forces spelled out in the

Peace Treaty and to "employ its best efforts to prevent any violation of its terms."[8]

The means at the disposal of the Force to implement its task, as outlined in Annex I of the Peace Treaty, are as follows:

a) the operation of checkpoints, reconnaissance patrols, and observation posts along the international boundary and line B, and within Zone C, to ensure that military elements or equipment of a military nature are not brought into Zone C;

b) periodic verification in the four Zones of the implementation of the provisions of the Annex (to be carried out not less than twice a month, unless otherwise agreed by the parties);

c) additional verifications within 48 hours after the receipt of a request from one of the parties;

The Force is to report its findings to both parties. If the MFO verifies that a violation indeed has taken place, the violating party must rectify it within 48 hours and notify the MFO. According to the Peace Treaty, these functions are to be implemented in Zones A, B and C by the Force and in Zone D (on the Israeli side of the international border, in the Negev) by observers.[9] Beyond what is stated in the Peace Treaty, the parties agreed in the Protocol that when a violation has been confirmed by the MFO, they will rectify it within 48 hours, and the party in question will notify the MFO of the rectification.[10] Moreover, while the Peace Treaty stipulated that periodic verifications were to be carried out by UN observers in Zone D and by UN Forces in Zones A, B and C,[11] under the new arrangement the parties agreed to form a unit of civilian observers for verification purposes in all the Zones, so that the military duties of the MFO are confined to Zone C.[12] Verifications are undertaken by the Force in Zone C, and by the Naval Unit in the Strait of Tiran (part of Zone C).

The Civilian Observer Unit (COU), consisting of some 25 US citizens, all civilians, is patterned after the SFM model. It is responsible for verifying troop strength, weaponry and military infrastructure throughout Zone A (adjoining the Suez Canal to the East; see map), Zone B (in the center sector), Zone C (where the MFO's military component is located), and Zone D (the narrow strip within Israel). Verifications are made periodically, not less than twice a month, by small teams of generally two or three civilian observers. They are accompanied by an Egyptian liaison officer in Zones A, B and C, and by an Israeli Defense Forces liaison officer in Zone D. They employ helicopters and a variety of ground transportation. Under MFO procedures a typical mission lasts about three days. During a complete cycle of missions, the observers visit all the military installations throughout the area of their mandate during the three days. The first day is for observation, during which they fly and locate all the military installations. On the second and third days they proceed with on-the-ground verifications. The monthly pattern now is that the Civilian Observer Unit conducts two air reconnaissances and two land verifications on alternate weeks. There are fixed, announced inspections, as well as unannounced random inspections. Inspection routes are largely routine, but some routes are chosen at random, with minimum advance notice to the parties.[13] As stated, in addition to these regular missions, the observers are also prepared to undertake additional "on the spot" verifications within 48 hours of a request from either party.[14] Such extra missions have thus far rarely been requested.

Within Zone C, as part of the ground regime the MFO military infantry battalions man the observation posts (OPs) and checkpoints (CPs) and conduct MFO air and ground patrols. Under the naval regime, the three Italian minesweepers sail from the Egyptian port of Sharm-El-Sheikh to patrol the international waterway of the Strait of Tiran. Finally, under the aerial regime, the MFO undertakes support flights to Egypt or Israel, verification flights in the Zones, and reconnaissance flights over Zone C.[15]

It has been pointed out that observation and patrolling in the Strait of Tiran have been more regular and energetic than elsewhere, and responses to suspicious incidents more rapid. Operationally, "ensuring" the freedom of navigation now means that the MFO would implement procedures for "containing the situation by calling on violators to cease and desist, relying on the Egyptians to remove the interference, but to do so themselves if this should be necessary."[16]

According to the Peace Treaty each party undertakes to prevent terrorist activity originating in its territory against the other party.[17] The MFO Protocol emphasizes that the operations of the Force shall not be construed as substituting for the undertakings of the parties in this regard. The MFO is charged with reporting such acts of violence, hostility and/or subversion by individuals, in the first instance to the police of the respective party.[18] Israeli officials have indicated that they expected the MFO not only to monitor adherence to the Peace Treaty, but also "to prevent by any means necessary any attempt by Palestinians to smuggle arms through Sinai into the Gaza Strip." Ariel Sharon, then Israeli Defense Minister, stated in March 1982 that the Israel Defense Forces (IDF) had seized some 500 grenades being smuggled on this route. A fatal grenade ambush of an Israeli vehicle in the Gaza Strip at that time appeared to indicate that some were nevertheless getting through.[19] It is difficult, however, to determine whether arms and ammunition are actually brought in from Egypt, or whether they are locally made or are part of old stockpiles. While this issue might become a problem, so far it has not been critical.

The only significant border dispute between Egypt and Israel that was not settled prior to Israel's final withdrawal on April 25, 1982 concerned fifteen disputed border points which include the small area of land at Taba. On April 25, Egypt and Israel signed a separate agreement (text unpublished but not secret) calling for further negotiations and settlement of the dispute according to Article 7 of the Peace Treaty. It is stated therein inter alia that the parties agreed to request the MFO to maintain security in the disputed areas, pending resolution of the problem.[20] With the outbreak of the Lebanon war in June 1982, Egypt tempered its relations with Israel, and no discussions regarding the MFO's entry into these areas took place for some time. An unsuccessful round of talks was held in Ismailiya in March 1983. The MFO was thus never deployed in Taba due to disagreements over its prospective role there, as Egypt and Israel failed to arrive at a common definition of its function "to maintain security."

The position of the MFO has been that though it is anxious to be helpful in resolving this dispute, an agreed upon definition of its security role must be reached by the parties themselves. A "security role in Taba would be a possible extension of the Protocol and the Peace Treaty," as these agreements did not envision disputes in border areas. As long as Egypt and Israel are unable to agree on the precise nature of the MFO's security role in regard to Taba, the Force is careful not to become involved.[21] According to the MFO Director-General, it was not a question of the parties not wanting the MFO in the area, but rather a question of what the MFO was to do there.[22]

At one point Egypt announced that it wished to discuss the question of the MFO's role in Taba not in the framework of the joint Israel-Egypt military committee, but in Rome, with the participation of the MFO directorate.[23]

At the end of 1984, Egypt proposed to Israel that the mandate of the MFO be extended for it to be deployed to police the Taba area.[24] A three-day round of talks was held at the end of January 1985 in Beersheba. The talks centered on the role of the MFO in the area.

Egypt demanded that Israel remove its police and Border Police from Taba and place the area in the charge of the MFO. (At the completion of the Sinai withdrawal, Israel had agreed to keep its troops out of the zone, leaving only police and Border Police.) The Egyptian position was that the presence of the Israeli police in the area was contrary to the agreement of April 25, 1982, stipulating that the MFO be responsible for Taba.[25] It wanted the MFO to replace Israeli police in all their functions, including day-to-day police functions to maintain law and order, until the final status of the area was determined.[26] As a matter of policy, Egypt seems to be interested in a strong MFO presence in the area, which it deems preferable to the Israeli police presence.

Israel's position was that its police and Border Police should continue functioning in the area, with the MFO role limited to the military task of "keeping foreign forces out."[27]   It does not consider the MFO to be appropriate for police functions.   The Beersheba meeting ended without producing a final document. It was understood that the talks would continue in the joint Israel-Egypt military committee.

Israel hoped that Egypt would be prepared to discuss Taba at a further meeting along with other disputed issues in an across-the-board effort to thaw the "cold peace." It soon emerged, however, that the Egyptian position remained that it was ready to discuss only the issue of Taba, whose final disposition, in its view, should be decided by arbitration. It was reported that Egypt was interested in the immediate introduction of the MFO to Taba. Israel first wished to ascertain the role of the MFO in the area, whether it would be merely symbolic or whether it would assume police functions. Egypt demanded the withdrawal of the Israeli police from the area, while Israel suggested that the police presence be converted to a tourism police.[28]

Another source of controversy has been over the number of battalions maintained by Egypt in Zone A. While the number of brigades and personnel in the area is regulated in the Peace Treaty military annex (see above), there is no indication of the number of battalions.   Israel has contended that the number of battalions stationed there by Egypt exceeds the accepted norm and the number previously maintained per brigade.   Israel's fear may be that each battalion could potentially serve as a nucleus for expanding Egyptian forces. As such, this violates the "spirit" of the Treaty and undermines the confidence-building role of the MFO.[29]

Military sources in Israel at one point assumed that US troops participating in the MFO would be used as a spearhead unit in case of US intervention in neighboring areas such as Saudi Arabia and Persian Gulf countries. These sources pointed out that the US soldiers participating in the MFO were part of the Rapid Deployment Force (RDF) set up earlier in the US. Israel strongly objected to any overlap between the MFO and the RDF, in order not to jeopardize the MFO, and Egypt apparently felt the same. US sources flatly rejected this theory, and maintained that the US soldiers would serve exclusively in Sinai. It was emphasized that US troops in the Sinai would not play any kind of broad strategic role in defending US interests in the Middle East and in the Gulf.[30] The Commander of the US battalion stated early on that he foresaw no change in his troops' mission and that they would act according to MFO instructions.

NOTES

(1) MFO Protocol, Art. 5; Annex, Art. 8.
(2) Appendix to Annex I, Art. 3.
(3) Appendix to Annex I, Art. 1, para. 2 (b).
(4) Ibid., Art. 2, para. 4.
(5) Ibid., Art. 4, para. 3 (b).
(6) For a detailed analysis of this function, see Lapidoth, pp. 376-77; id., "The Strait of Tiran, the Gulf of Aqaba, and the 1979 Treaty of Peace between Egypt and Israel," 70 Am. J. Int'l L. 84-108, at 104 (1983); Peace Treaty, Art. 5; Annex I, Art. 4; MFO Annex, Art. 10 (d).
(7) Peace Treaty, Annex I, Art. 2 ("Determination of Final Lines and Zones"), para. 1.
(8) MFO Annex, Art. 9. For details, see Lapidoth, pp. 376-77. See supra Ch. 3, note 41.
(9) Peace Treaty, Annex I, Art. 6.
(10) MFO Annex, Art. 11.
(11) Peace Treaty, Annex I, Art. 6, para. 3.
(12) "The Multinational Force" (Hebrew), Ma'arachot (No. 283) 28 (July 1982).
(13) MFO Annual Report, 1984, p. 18. Alan James, "Symbol in Sinai: The Multinational Force and Observers" (mimeo) 16 (July 11, 1984).
(14) Transcript of Press Conference by MFO Director-General, Mr. Hunt, with Rome Representatives of International Wire Services, Rome, January 17, 1983 (hereinafter: Hunt Press Conference, Jan. 17, 1983), p. 3; MFO Annual Report, 1983, p. 26.
(15) MFO Annex, Arts. 15, 16, 18.
(16) Pelcovits, p. 75. The regime of Zone C extends over the Islands of Tiran and Sanafir at the entrance of the Gulf of Aqaba. See James, pp. 10, 21.
(17) Art. 3, para. 2.
(18) MFO Annex, Art. 12. The MFO does not check cars; according to an MFO official it has no right to do so (Interview, Dec. 9, 1984).

(19) Jerusalem Post Magazine, April 2, 1982, p. 6. Pelcovits, pp. 76-77.

The Convention on the Prohibition or Restriction on the Use of Certain Conventional Weapons which May Be Deemed Excessively Injurious or to Have Indiscriminate Effects provides that the parties shall retain records of the location of minefields, mines and booby-traps, and "when a United Nations force or mission performs functions in any area, [it shall] make available to the authority mentioned in Article 8 such information as is required by that Article;" (Art. 7 (3b)).

Article 8
Protection of United Nations forces and missions from the effects of minefields, mines and booby-traps

1. "When a United Nations force or mission performs functions of peacekeeping, observation or similar functions in any area, each party to the conflict shall, if requested by the head of the United Nations force or mission in that area, as far as it is able:
(a) remove or render harmless all mines or booby traps in that area;
(b) take such measures as may be necessary to protect the force or mission from the effects of minefields, mines and booby traps while carrying out its duties; and
(c) make available to the head of the United Nations force or mission in that area, all information in the party's possession concerning the location of minefields, mines and booby traps in that area."

19 Int'l Legal Materials (No. 6) 1532, at 1533-34 (Nov. 1980).

(20) The April 25, 1982 agreement stipulates that "activities which have been conducted in these areas shall continue. No new construction projects will be initiated in these areas." An Israeli hotel that had been started before the agreement has since been completed in Taba. Jerusalem Post, March 19, 1982, p. 2.

On Taba see Jerusalem Post, April 27, 1982, p. 1. New York Times, March 25, 1984, p. 14. Jerusalem Post, Nov. 30, 1982, p. 1.

(21) Hunt Press Conference, Jan. 17, 1983, pp. 7-8.

(22) UPA, Cairo, Nov. 29, 1982, reported in Haaretz, Nov. 30, 1982, p. 2.

(23) Ma'ariv, Nov. 30, 1984, p. 2.

(24) Jerusalem Post, Dec. 28, 1984, p. 2.

(25) Jerusalem Post, Jan. 28, 1985, p. 1.

(26) According to Egyptian officials the MFO presence in Taba would be an interim measure, pending resolution of the territorial issue by conciliation or arbitration according to the provisions of the Peace Treaty. (Jerusalem Post, Jan. 25, 1985, p. 2.) Egypt considers the MFO presence in Taba to be an interim issue, pending the settlement of the disputed long-range sovreignty issue. It called for arbitration to rule on which of the two States rightfully owns Taba, arguing that negotiations have

proven fruitless. The Israeli view was that "negotiations have not yet been exhausted, and that even if they have been, the first recourse should be conciliation, and only should that fail, the question would go to arbitration." (Jerusalem Post, Jan. 27, 1985, p. 2.) It was reported that Israel had proposed issuing a statement that the presence of Israeli police would not prejudice claims to ownership. (Jerusalem Post, Jan. 29, 1985, p. 1.) Israel proposed that a special procedural committee should be formed, to be charged with deciding all the details relative to conciliation or arbitration, which are both provided for in Article 7 of the Peace Treaty. "Israel wants conciliation, not arbitration, because in arbitration the parties must commit themselves in advance to accepting the arbitrator's ruling." (Jerusalem Post, Jan. 30, 1985, p. 1.) For background see Moshe Sharon, "Tangle over Taba," Jerusalem Post, Feb. 1, 1985, p. 7; Thomas L. Friedman, New York Times, News of the Week in Review, Feb. 3, 1985, p. E5. Charles Rousseau, 86 Revue Générale de Droit International Public 787-89 (1982); 87 ibid., 654 (1983).

(27) Jerusalem Post, Jan. 28, 1985, p. 2.

(28) Jerusalem Post, April 5, 1985; Hazofe, April 7, 1985, p. 1.

(29) Interview with MFO official, Dec. 9, 1984. See Pelcovits, pp. 77-78.

(30) MFO House Hearings, p. 26. This was also a source of concern for some of the contributing States; see, e.g., 52 Australian Foreign Affairs Record (No. 11) 574 (Nov. 1981).

The second Operation Bright Star to test the RDF was held in November 1981 with the participation of the US, Egypt, Oman, Sudan and Somalia.

5
Structure and Organization

Considerable originality and innovation were required in order to design "from scratch" an apparatus that would organize and oversee the new international force. The organizers were presumably interested in shaping the MFO into an independently functioning multinational entity. Understandably, Egypt and Israel may have had reason to be concerned about the force enjoying too much independence. The force itself could be modeled on the prototype of UN forces, but in the absence of an institutional superstructure like the UN Secretariat, a new international institution had to be molded, with a command structure formulated, and with operating procedures and rules of engagement drawn up.

Thus, in many regards, inventiveness was used in establishing the structure of the force. The basic operational concept of the MFO was developed through a series of three-party (Egypt, Israel and the US) and later four-party (including the MFO) discussions.

Responsibilities within the MFO are divided among four units: MFO Headquarters in Rome, Force Headquarters in the Sinai, and the offices of the Director-General's Representatives in Cairo and Tel Aviv.

The purpose of this chapter is to describe the structure of the MFO and how it is organized to carry out its functions effectively.

THE DIRECTOR-GENERAL

Given the lack of a pre-existing superstructure (as in the UN system) to organize and supervise the MFO, an original organ was required to ensure the functioning of the Force and the performance of its tasks. Likewise, it was necessary to designate an authority which would appoint a commander and take care of related matters: the budget, recruitment, logistics, etc. It was agreed, therefore, to appoint a civilian Director-General of US citizenship, who would work together with representatives of Egypt and Israel, as a political administrative body.

As stated, Mr. Leamon R. Hunt (formerly the Director of the US Sinai Field Mission, 1977-79) was appointed by Egypt and Israel, upon the suggestion of the US, as MFO interim Director-General. Following ratification of the Protocol the parties made his appointment permanent.[1] Hunt was fatally shot in Rome on February 15, 1984 by a group that wanted "imperialist forces out of Lebanon" and Italy out of NATO. Victor H. Dikeos, a retired US diplomat served as interim Director-General[2] until Peter D. Constable assumed duties as the Director-General on September 1, 1984.

The Director-General is appointed for a four-year term. This term is renewable, but it may also be curtailed by the parties. He is responsible for the direction of the MFO in fulfilling its functions. In this capacity he is authorized to act on behalf of the Force, to engage a sufficient number of staff, to institute legal proceedings, to contract, to acquire and dispose of property, and to take such actions as are required for the fulfillment of his responsibilities. He is to report to the parties on developments relating to the functioning of the MFO, and in this regard, he may raise any matter with the parties.[3]

The Director-General and his staff handle all diplomatic matters among the MFO and Egypt and Israel, as well as with the governments of the Participating States. The Director-General's functions in some ways are similar to those of the UN Secretary-General: he invites contributors to participate in the

Force and coordinates the nature of their participation with them.

Overall financial control is an important function of the Rome Headquarters. The Director-General formulates and presents the MFO budget, exercises financial control, and directs MFO operations involving contracts, procurement, property management, claims and disputes.

Cases of violations or disagreements between the two sides are referred to the Director-General. Unlike the UN Secretary-General, the MFO Director-General is not a representative of an institution with its own prestige and legitimacy on the one hand, and biases and constraints on the other. To a large extent, he must establish his own authority, through his own talents and initiatives. These may run counter to the sensitivities of the parties. His personal stature and discretion will largely determine the success of his performance. Both the Director-General and the Commander of the MFO are basically on their own in carrying out their tasks and ensuring that the MFO implements its responsibilities.

THE COMMANDER AND MILITARY COMMAND STRUCTURE

The Commander of the Force is appointed by the Director-General, subject to the approval of the parties, who may renew or curtail his three-year term. He must be an officer with the rank of general and not of the same nationality as the Director-General.

The Commander has full command authority over the Force and is responsible for its daily command. He is in charge of maintaining the good order of the Force. It is his responsibility to report any violation of the Peace Treaty's security arrangements to the Director-General and to both parties.[4] The Commander is to promulgate the Standing Operating Procedures (SOPs) of the Force. The SOPs were developed by General Bull-Hansen. They are a military translation of the MFO Protocol. They regulate the behavior of the Force, the behavior of the troops while on vacation, and set down the rules of the Force.

As pointed out by Professor Ruth Lapidoth, formulation of the

SOPs is an important power delegated to the Commander, as these procedures include the equivalent of rules of engagement, namely, guidelines for how the Force is to react in the event that hostilities break out, as well as when and under what circumstances to use force.[5] The Commander is to report his findings simultaneously to the parties as soon as possible, but not later than 24 hours after a verification or after a violation has been confirmed. He is also to provide the parties simultaneously with a monthly report summarizing the findings of the checkpoints, observation posts and reconnaissance patrols.[6]

The Force Commander's staff is composed of officers from all the participating States. It is organized to provide the different areas of expertise required for a modern military organization with peacekeeping duties.

The Commander is to establish a chain of command for the MFO linked to the commanders of the national contingents. Although remaining in their national service, MFO members, during their period of service to the Force, are "under the Director-General and subject to the authority of the Commander through the chain of command." While the Commander is generally responsible for disciplinary action in national contingents, direct responsibility for disciplinary action in national contingents participating in the MFO rests with the individual commanders of those contingents.[7]

The post of Commander was first held by Lieutenant-General Frederik V. Bull-Hansen of Norway, who in 1956-57 served as a captain at UNEF-I headquarters in Sinai. On March 27, 1984, Lieutenant-General Egil J. Ingebrigtsen, another Norwegian senior officer, replaced Bull-Hansen, who became Norwegian Chief of Defense. Ingebrigtsen, a veteran UN officer, served with UNTSO in northern Israel in the 1970s.

THE FORCE

The Force's three infantry battalions, as specified in the Protocol (Annex, Art. 19), total not more than 2000 troops. As stated, the Civilian Observer Unit, as well as the various military support units, employ approximately another 600 military and 800 civilian personnel of Egyptian and other nationalities.[8] It has been pointed out that the functions established for the Force could be carried out by fewer than the actual number of men involved. However, besides the personnel verifying compliance with the Peace Treaty, the parties wanted the physical presence of a larger force to act as deterrent.

The troops are generally rotated every six months, since they work in desert conditions. However, as stated, the Fijian battalion, by a decision of the Fijian Government, and members of the Force Commander's staff, "in the interest of executive efficiency and operational continuity," serve for one year. Civilian tours of duty in Sinai vary in length.[9]

The Military

The MFO military forces, as stated, remain in Zone C. The operational arm of the military forces consists of light infantry battalions from Colombia, Fiji and the US, and the Naval Coastal Patrol Unit from Italy. Transport, communications and logistic support is provided by other contingents.

The structure of the Force is as follows:

- A headquarters unit (headed by the Commander) at El Gorah. It includes representatives of all the participating States, a British headquarters company and three Norwegian officers.
- Three infantry divisions (battalions--about 2000 persons): The US based at Sharm-El-Sheikh (deployed at the Gulf of Aqaba); Colombia (central sector); and Fiji (northern sector). The latter two are based at El Gorah.
- An aerial unit equipped with light planes and helicopters for surveillance.
    a) Australian helicopters with a crew of 99 Australians, 40 men from New Zealand, based at El Gorah;
    b) 10 US helicopters -- part of its battalion; operating

from Sharm-El-Sheikh airbase;

c)   3 transport planes (French).

- A naval unit (Italian), equipped with three minesweepers to supervise freedom of navigation in the Strait of Tiran and the Gulf of Aqaba (based at Sharm-El-Sheikh).
- A military police unit (the Netherlands).
- A signals unit (some 70 soldiers from Holland).
- A logistics unit in charge of providing services and supplies to the Force (350 soldiers from the US; a 75-man transportation unit from Uruguay. As stated, at the MFO's request, in March 1983, Uruguay replaced 35 of its motor transport personnel with engineering specialists charged with maintaining the MFO's road network).

The Observers

Initially the Civilian Observer Unit (COU) had some organizational advantage over other MFO personnel, as its members had transferred as a group from the US Sinai Field Mission (SFM). From April 1980 to April 1982 the SFM had carried out limited verification missions similar to those required of the MFO.

As stated, the Civilian Observers Unit is in charge of supervising on the Israeli side of the border (Zone D) and verifying the security arrangements in all four Zones (in Zone C, in addition, the three battalions of the military forces operate observation posts, patrols and helicopters). Typically on a verification mission the Observers inquire how many personnel are on location, to which unit they belong, and ask to see their weapons.

The Observers are people with State Department (or related foreign affairs agencies) or military experience. A pair of Observers is always accompanied by a liaison officer from the armed forces of the party whose territory is being inspected.[10]

LIAISON

For the purpose of consultations, assessment of progress and resolution of problems, the parties appoint senior officials to serve as liaison officers with the Director-General. The permanent representatives of the Director-General at the MFO offices in Cairo and Tel Aviv maintain contacts with the Egyptian and Israeli liaison systems respectively and with other national authorities in each State as necessary. The system is designed to prevent situations resulting from errors or misinterpretations on the part of either party.[11]

In practice, under the liaison system, military officers from the MFO Commander's staff meet almost daily with their Egyptian and Israeli counterparts. The Egyptian liaison group was headed by Rear-Admiral Hamdy, and later by Brigadier-General Farouk Ahmed Labib, and the Israeli group by Brigadier-General Dov Sion. The system provides a mechanism whereby the MFO and the two parties can maintain constant and rapid communications on matters relating to the MFO peacekeeping mission. Such matters include reports by the Force Commander on verification missions completed and any violations of Peace Treaty provisions that may occur. These reports are made exclusively to the two parties and to the Director-General.[12] Active daily contact is maintained regarding possible violations and infiltrations during the previous night, involving notification by telex and on the spot checks, and the processing of MFO personnel crossing the border.

As pointed out by Pelcovits, "the procedures developed by the MFO stress the diplomacy of reconciling differences at the force commander's level, with the director-general intervening only as needed. Contested matters rarely are brought to the foreign offices, let alone to the ministers."[13]

LOCATION OF THE MFO

The Peace Treaty and Protocol do not provide details regarding the deployment of the MFO within Zone C. The main bases were to be in the areas of Rafah and Sharm-El-Sheikh.[14] The checkpoints, reconnaissance patrols and observation posts are to operate along the international boundary and Line B, and within Zone C.[15]

Already in April 1981, a survey team visited various sites in Zone C in the Sinai in order to formulate recommendations for the location of the two main bases. (These are called "camps" by the MFO, in deference to Egypt's sensitivity regarding the term "base."[16]) Other teams then visited the desert for initial design planning. By July agreement had been reached on the location of the MFO's two main bases. Egypt had opposed the location of bases in populated areas. Therefore the MFO's North Base and Sinai Headquarters were designated at El Gorah, which was still the site of Israel's Eitam Air Base. The choice of Eitam over Etzion, located halfway south in the Sinai and more centrally situated, was made by the MFO, with Egyptian acquiescence.

Although the Eitam air base was outside the area designated in the Peace Treaty for the stationing of UN forces, Israel agreed to its serving as the main MFO base for practical reasons and as an additional guarantee that Egypt would refrain from using the air base for military purposes.[17]

The South Base and port facility for the Naval Coastal Patrol Unit was designated at a new camp south of the Na'ama Bay, north of Sharm-El-Sheikh (Ophira), at the southern tip of the peninsula on the Red Sea shore.[18] Stationing the US battalion in the south may have been the result of strong Israeli pressure, "possibly reflecting the calculation that in the event of a crisis between Egypt and herself the Americans would both be at a critical strategic spot and largely out of the Israeli line of fire."[19]

In August 1981 the MFO opened an office in Tel Aviv, the closest major city to the construction sites in the Sinai. Since only seven months remained until March 1982 when the MFO forces were to be in place in the Sinai, on August 31 the Director-General signed an agreement with the US Army Corps of Engineers, which was designated as the MFO's construction agent, in order to ensure the best available expertise on "fast track" construction of military facilities.[20]

The MFO Commander was responsible for the location of checkpoints and observation posts. The checkpoints were placed along the international boundary and on line B along main arteries leading to Zone C. Observation posts were established at dominant points within Zone C and on the Island of Tiran, and provided with access roads. A total of 40 remote sites, including sector control centers, were established.[21] A main supply route from North to South, based partly on existing roads, had to be completed.

In all, the MFO has constructed over a hundred million dollars worth of facilities for the Force in the desert. These include military base facilities, roads throughout the area, as well as some 40 observation posts and checkpoints with housing, supply and logistic facilities for groups of generally twelve to fifteen persons at each location.[22]

The Director-General has the right to establish the location of his office, subject to the consent of the host country.[23] This provision "reflects the determination of the negotiators that the civilian leadership of the MFO be located outside the treaty area."[24] The Director-General initially established a temporary headquarters in Alexandria, Virginia. Meanwhile, the MFO began a search for a permanent location in a city closer to the Sinai which could provide good transportation and communication links. Eventually these conditions were fulfilled when the Italian Government extended an invitation to establish MFO headquarters in Rome. In November 1982, the Dirctor-General and his staff completed the move from their temporary offices in Virginia to the permanent Rome headquarters. From that city the Director-General and a group of about thirty officials from various countries exercise general administrative and policy supervision over MFO activities and keep in touch with the Governments of Egypt, Israel and the participating States.[25]

On April 25, 1981, the temporary offices that the MFO had

established in Cairo and Tel Aviv to supervise construction, logistic and administrative matters became the offices of the Director-General's permanent representatives in those two cities. In the course of earlier planning it had become clear that the MFO would require a mechanism to handle policy and administrative matters not covered by the liaison system. Richard Smith in Cairo and Robert Miller in Tel Aviv serve as the Director-General's personal representatives to the Governments of Egypt and Israel respectively, as well as to the diplomatic missions of the participating States in those countries. These offices also carry out administrative support functions, especially in the procurement, contracting and personnel areas.[26]

Operational control over the Force is from the main headquarters at El Gorah, aided by several sector control centers. The MFO has its own independent sophisticated communications system linking the main and secondary headquarters and each field post, vehicle and aircraft. A French fixed-wing airplane flies between the two main headquarters. The MFO also has telephone and teleprinter connection links with Israeli and Egyptian liaison headquarters.

MILITARY POLICE

The Director-General designates military police to police the premises of the MFO and the areas where the Force operates.

The military police of the MFO must immediately transfer to the civilian police of the Receiving State any individual who is not a member of the MFO, who it takes into custody. The police of the Receiving State must immediately transfer to the MFO any member of the MFO who it takes into temporary custody, pending a determination concerning jurisdiction.[27]

ARMAMENTS AND USE OF FORCE

The Peace Treaty does not deal with the subject of weapons for the Force. Israel wanted the MFO to be equipped with reasonable arms, meaning that units would not be deprived of their natural weapons. For example, if a battalion had four mortars in a support company, it should be able to keep them and not be stripped of its natural support. Egypt, on the other hand, wanted the Force to have almost no arms, or "light armaments." According to the compromise reached in the MFO Protocol, "The MFO units will have standard armaments and equipment appropriate to their peacekeeping mission as stipulated in this Annex."[28] It is questionable whether in this formulation the word "standard" applies only to armaments or to equipment as well.

In practice, the MFO would be unable to carry out military activity against a party guilty of violating the Peace Treaty. As stated, the weapons for MFO troops consist of M-16 rifles, and Mouser rifles for the Colombians. Thus, in effect, the MFO does not possess the means to enforce the security arrangements under the Peace Treaty. For example, there is no MFO air surveillance and no radar. The arms carried by the members of the peacekeeping operation are intended only for self-defense and the rules governing the use of force are very restrictive. Every military member is issued a Use of Force Instruction Card, with the following guidelines:

> Your principal duty as a member of the MFO is to observe and report. You are armed with your individual weapon for self protection. The firing of your weapon at another individual will be done only as a last resort and to protect your life or the life of another member of the MFO. Never use more force than necessary. Whenever possible request orders from your commander before you use force.[29]

Basically, the rules of engagement (which are posted) state that even if fired upon, shoot only if your life is threatened, and shoot not to kill. If you can drive away, do not shoot.

LOGISTICS[30]

Due to its desert setting and politically sensitive surroundings, the MFO's logistic support function is "a very special operation, presenting problems and solutions that do not always follow standard logistic doctrine."

> From the outset, the MFO logistics system has represented a substantial improvement over traditional multinational systems. Many peacekeeping forces have in the past used a system based on the principle that one nation, often called the core-nation, would provide the framework and fundamental input of their logistics. While the MFO logistics system was planned on a similar pattern and used the U.S. Department of Defense logistical systems, it also relies on commercial supply and other national systems.[31]

From its inception, the MFO organized a system of centralized purchasing and equipment standardization. The principle underlying MFO logistics was that each unit, regardless of its resources, should receive the same type of equipment. The advantage of this system is that it promotes fairness and efficiency. This is in contrast with the system used in UN peacekeeping operations, where a variety of equipment and maintenance standards are often found in different contingents.

A large percentage of the MFO's supplies come from the US through the Department of Defense supply system or civilian procurement by the MFO. Items coming from the US average more than 90 days en route. Initially only about 15 percent of the supplies were obtained from Egypt or Israel. There is now a tendency to purchase more products locally in Egypt and Israel.

Logistical support includes base camp support and field logistics. The center of support operations is the North Base Camp, where the force headquarters, Logistical Support Unit (LSU) and support contractor are located. Similar support is provided at the South Base Camp at a reduced level. Logistical operations are performed by individual contingents, the LSU and a support contractor.

Each of the 24 observation posts, 14 checkpoints and five sector control centers in the network in Zone C comprises sleeping and living quarters, communications rooms, and in some cases communications shelters. Power is supplied by electrical generators, and there is stored fuel and water at each location. Sector support sites located with selected observation posts are situated along the main supply route where they can be resupplied by the LSU and in turn provide additional fuel and water to the other locations.

The main operator of the logistic system is the Logistical Support Unit (LSU), which, as stated, is a US combat service support organization. It consists of about 350 personnel drawn from various support units throughout the US. It is divided into five companies: headquarters, support, medical, transportation and the LSU South Camp detachment. They perform the following logistical services:

- line haul cargo from ports;
- operate depots for all classes of supply;
- provide fuel points at both base camps;
- line haul fuel and water to sector support sites;
- operate a movement control center;
- provide maintenance;
- provide explosive ordnance disposal;
- operate medical dispensaries at both base camps; and
- operate Army post office and finance (for US personnel).

The support contractor provides the MFO with an approximately 200-man multinational expatriate labor force, augmented as available by Egyptian personnel. These workers, divided between the two main base camps perform various logistical functions:

- operate the multinational dining facility at El Gorah;
- provide second and third-level vehicle maintenance;
- maintain the commercial radio equipment and telephone system;
- provide custodial services;
- operate power generators for the base camps;
- operate the laundry, barber, tailor and force exchange;
- provide fire sevice; and
- provide the commercial procurement of supplies.

FINANCING

The effective functioning of an international force is contingent upon smooth and adequate financing. Those who finance the Force -- the parties in the case of the MFO -- have an interest in keeping the costs down. The participants are interested in good conditions for their troops, and the MFO must balance these considerations without permitting interference in its day-to-day financial decisions.

For the initial period (July 17, 1981 to September 30, 1982), during which exceptional expenses were anticipated in connection with the establishment of the Force, the US agreed to provide three-fifths of the costs. (The US was to be reimbursed by the MFO for the costs incurred in the change of station of US Armed Forces provided to the MFO and for the costs of providing civilian observers to the MFO.) Accordingly, during that period Israel and Egypt each paid 20 percent of the costs. After the initial year, the US committed itself to contributing one-third of the MFO's annual operating expenses (subject to the same understanding on reimbursements).[32]

The MFO Protocol stipulates that the expenses of the Force which are not covered by other sources shall be borne equally by the parties.[33] Thus Egypt and Israel each pays one-third of the expenses.

The budget for each financial year is prepared by the Director-General and must be approved by the parties.[34] The US pays for the surveillance flights. It participates in the budget discussions.

The MFO budget for the first financial year (September 9, 1981 through September 1982) was over $200 million in direct expenditures, of which approximately $100 million was for building and facilities. Understandably, the initial budget was heavy on fixed assets. The operating expenditure was approximately $100 million.[35]

The anticipated budget for 1983 and 1984 was about $110 million, and $100 million for 1985. MFO budgets take into account the

level of inflation. This "direct funding," as stated, is split
evenly three ways between the US, Egypt and Israel. (See Financial
Statement in Appendix.) For 1982-83, the MFO was able to reimburse
about $5 million to each of the three countries. For 1983-84,
about $7-8 million each were to be refunded. These refunds were
possible due to fluctuations in exchange rates, purchasing in
countries with lowest prices, and savings through gained
experience. Due to inflation, a large part of the budget is now
allocated to personnel. Much less is now spent on food, due to the
elimination of waste, adjustment to the taste of each contingent, a
shorter supply line (a warehouse in Ashdod, Israel, was eliminated)
and stricter reliance on local purchases rather than on imports.
Most of the problems discussed at the semi-annual meetings in Rome
between the parties involved deal with money. For example, one of
the questions raised is why should one side pay the consumer tax on
products purchased in the country of the other party?[36]

The term "direct funding" denotes cash contributions made in
response to MFO budget estimates of future operating and
maintenance costs. There are, however, significant financial
contributions made by all the participating States, some of which
may be viewed as direct funding. The ten participating States, as
well as Norway, are contributing personnel; five are also
contributing capital equipment. In negotiating most of the
participation agreements, the basic formula applied was that the
contributing State would bear those ordinary costs of troop
maintenance that would be paid at home, while the MFO would absorb
the extraordinary costs associated with service in the Sinai.
France, for example, pays the basic salary of her airmen, i.e. the
allowances they would draw if they were serving in France. The MFO
pays for their transportation and maintenance and the extra costs
and allowances of having them in the Sinai. This formula was
modified somewhat for those governments facing heavy financial
commitments.[37]

The use of capital equipment is in effect a significant
additional form of direct support by some of the participating
States. The MFO reimburses those countries contributing capital

equipment for the maintenance and use of that equipment. For example, Italy contributes three minesweepers, which are very expensive. Australia and New Zealand contribute helicopters, and France fixed wing airplanes. By a special arrangement, the US provides its own jeeps, trucks and much of its own battalion equipment. This relieves the MFO of having to purchase that equipment.[38] Initially a report of the General Accounting Office to Congress expressed the fear that the US might be forced into greater than planned contributions of troops to Sinai. The US contribution over the first two and a half years was expected to cost $170 million. The surveillance flights which the US pledged to continue were expected to cost $8 million a year.[39]

The method of financing constitutes one of the fundamental differences between UN forces and the MFO. Forces such as UNEF-I and ONUC were financed by the rough division of costs between the participating States and the UN.[40] As is well known from the ICJ advisory opinion on "Certain Expenses of the United Nations," some members refused to pay their share of the cost in these operations, and this caused protracted strife in the Organization.[41] In the case of the MFO, the parties to the Peace Treaty and the United States, by being responsible for the financial support of the Force, have a strong stake in its success. On the other hand, the participating States in the case of the MFO invest their manpower, equipment and prestige, but are not burdened by the overall direct financing. A further difference is that UN peacekeeping operations have their administrative overhead paid for under the general UN assessment, whereas the MFO had to start from scratch and pay for everything.

According to some estimates, the MFO is the most expensive of any peacekeeping operation ever.[42] Indeed, the parties may have some room for concern over the high costs and over whether the Force is worth the expense. When the costs are weighed against the advantages derived from the MFO's method of financing and operations, however, the benefits clearly seem to justify the price. Assured financing based on direct funding by the parties and the US has facilitated the recruitment of contingents from

States that are dependent on full and immediate reimbursement. Since the parties and the US contribute cash according to MFO budget estimates (which is then drawn upon on an equal basis among the three), the system is reliable and prevents the deficits that have plagued UN forces. Prompt payment by all three financial contributors permits the MFO to fulfill its functions without uncertainty in this regard. Finally, accountability to the parties ensures responsible spending by the MFO without excessive constraints in decision-making.

UNIFORMS AND IDENTIFICATION

All military units participating in the MFO wear their national uniforms. They all share a terracotta-red beret and an MFO sleeve-emblem depicting a dove and olive branches. The Observers wear easily identifiable red suits. MFO service vehicles, boats and aircraft do not carry the marks or license plates of any participating State, but the distinctive MFO identification mark and license.[43]

DUTIES OF MFO MEMBERS

Members of the MFO are duty-bound to respect the laws and regulations of the Receiving State and to refrain from any activity of a political character in the Receiving State and "from any action incompatible with the international nature of their duties or inconsistent with the spirit" of the MFO Protocol. In the performance of their duties, MFO members shall receive their instructions only from the Director-General and the chain of command he designates. MFO personnel are expected to exercise the utmost discretion concerning all matters related to their duties and functions. They must not communicate to anyone any information they know by virtue of their position with the MFO that has not been made public, except in the course of their duties or by authorization of the Director-General. These obligations do not cease upon the termination of their assignment wih the MFO.[44]

While outside the areas where they are functioning, members of the MFO must wear civilian dress, and when off-duty there they must not carry arms.[45] Vehicles bearing licence plates of the MFO must carry third party liability insurance.[46] Participating States may not acquire immovable property in the Receiving State without the agreement of the Government of the Receiving State.[47]

As pointed out by Nathan Pelcovits, the MFO has benefited from "its ability to create new institutional procedures free of the United Nations' bureaucratic encrustration and the cumbersomeness typical of long-established institutional procedures. ... On balance, the MFO has demonstrated that a fledgling institution is capable of introducing novel and creative ideas into international peacekeeping, particularly in logistics."[48]

NOTES

(1) MFO Protocol, Art. 6.
(2) New York Times, Feb. 16, 1984, p. 1; Feb. 22, 1984, p. 1.
(3) MFO Annex, Arts. 1-4. See also infra Ch. 6, at notes 32, 34.
(4) MFO Protocol, Art. 6. MFO Annex, Arts. 5, 6. MFO Annual Report, 1984, p. 14.
(5) MFO House Hearings, pp. 7-8. Lapidoth p. 378 at n. 27. See below, Section on Armaments and Use of Force.
(6) MFO Annex, Art. 22. Reporting formats were worked out by the Commander with the parties in the Joint Commission. Reports to the parties are transmitted to the liaison offices. Ibid., Art. 23.
(7) MFO Protocol, Art. 6; MFO Annex, Arts. 5-7. See Peace Treaty, Annex I, Art. 6, para. 9.
(8) MFO "Background and Mission" 4 (Rome, Nov. 17, 1982) (mimeo); Jerusalem Post, April 22, 1983, p. 7. MFO House Hearings, p. 63.
(9) Hunt Press Conference, Jan. 17, 1983, p. 10; MFO Annual Report, 1983, p. 30.
(10) James, p. 16.
(11) See Peace Treaty, Annex I, Arts. 6 (4), 7; Appendix to Annex I, Art. 4; MFO Annex, Arts. 31-32.
(12) MFO Annual Report, 1983, pp. 27-28.
(13) Pelcovits, p. 87.

(14) Dotted line areas designated on Map 1 of the Peace Treaty.

(15) Peace Treaty, Annex I, Art. 6, para. 2(a).

(16) James, p. 11.

(17) "The Multinational Force" (Hebrew), Ma'arachot (No. 283) 28 (July 1982).

(18) MFO Annual Report, 1983, p. 13. Work on the latter began in November 1981.

(19) James, p. 11.

(20) For details on construction of MFO facilities, see MFO Annual Report, 1983, pp. 13-14, 21 ff.

(21) Ibid. Ma'arachot, supra note 17, p. 29.

(22) Hunt Press Conference, Jan. 17, 1983, p. 3. For details see MFO Annual Report, 1983, p. 21.

(23) MFO Annex, Art. 2.

(24) MFO Annual Report, 1983, p. 9.

(25) Ibid., p. 29.

(26) Ibid., p. 28. MFO Annual Report, 1984, p. 14.

(27) MFO Appendix, Arts. 14, 15, 16.

(28) MFO Annex, Art. 20.

(29) Cornelis Homan, "MFO: Peacekeeping in the Middle East," 63 Military Review (No. 9) 2, at 13 (Sept. 1983). The rules of engagement, which have not been published, are similar to those of UN forces.

(30) This section is derived from ibid., pp. 9-10.

(31) MFO Annual Report, 1984, p. 20.

(32) Identical letters from the US to Egypt and Israel, Aug. 3, 1981, para. 3B. See MFO House Hearings, pp. 3-4; P.L. 97-132, Secs. 4, 5, 6(b) (3-6), (c)(2); 3 U.S. Code Congressional and Administrative News, 97th Congress, 1st Sess. (1981), pp. 2744-47.

(33) MFO Protocol, Art. 7. For details of financing, administration and facilities, see MFO Annex, Arts. 24-27.

(34) MFO Annex, Art. 24.

(35) MFO Annual Report, 1983, p. 12. MFO Annual Report, 1984, pp. 36, 13. Hunt Press Conference, Jan. 17, 1983, pp. 8-9. Hirsh Goodman, Jerusalem Post, Feb. 3, 1984, p. 1

(36) Interview with MFO official, Dec. 9, 1984.

(37) MFO Annual Report, 1983, p. 12. See, e.g. the document describing "Financial Arrangements" for the Australian contingent in 53 Australian Foreign Affairs Record (No. 2) 135-36 (Feb. 1982).

(38) Hunt Press Conference, Jan. 17, 1983, p. 9. There has been at least one shooting incident in the MFO: a private US contractor was shot in the southern part of the Colombian sector.

(39) Aviation Week & Space Technology, Sept. 21, 1981, p. 23. On the cost of MFO participation to the US see MFO House Hearings, pp. 28-31, 55-56, 68-69, 71 & Appendix 8 at 185; Pelcovits, p. 73.

(40) D.W. Bowett, United Nations Forces 139 (London 1964).

(41) [1962] I.C.J. Reports 170.

(42) According to Pelcovits (p. 92), operating and maintenance costs in the MFO are about $34,000 per person. This compares with $30,000 for UNIFIL, $26,000 for UNDOF and $12,000 for UNFICYP (where some battalions absorb the costs). For details on financing, see generally Pelcovits, pp. 89-92.

The costs of the UNEF-II, UNDOF and UNIFIL operations are estimated at $973 million. This is besides the costs for planning the operational and logistical support and for moving the forces into place. By the end of 1982, the deficit for UNEF-II and UNDOF was $62.2 million and for UNIFIL $143.7 million. (Roger A. Brooks, "U.N. Peacekeeping: An Empty Mandate," Heritage Foundation Backgrounder (No. 262) 6, 16-17 (April 29, 1983).) According to Brooks, a year's operating expenses for UNIFIL is $180 million; in 1982 the US contributed about $54.5 million, or about 32%. According to Wiseman, from its inception in March 1978 to June 1982 UNIFIL costs amounted to $449,889,727. (Henry Wiseman, "United Nations Peacekeeping: An Historical Overview," in Peacekeeping: Appraisals and Proposals 52 (Henry Wiseman ed. N.Y. 1983).)

(43) MFO Annex, Art. 21.
(44) MFO Appendix, Art. 6.
(45) Ibid., Arts. 21, 22.
(46) Ibid., Art. 32.
(47) Ibid., Art. 23.
(48) Pelcovits, p. 87.

6
Privileges and Immunities

Historically, UN forces in and around Israel were always interested in concluding an agreement regarding their immunities. Israel, being wary of UN forces, was reluctant to enter into such agreement, especially as regards immunity from criminal jurisdiction for arms and drug smuggling. Prior to the MFO agreement, Israel had never entered into an immunities agreement either with the UN or with States participating in a UN force. (Israel is a party to the 1946 Convention on Privileges and Immunities of the UN since 1949, but it has applied this Convention only with regard to UNTSO observers, in their role as "experts" as defined in the Convention.) In the absence of an agreement providing for immunities, foreign troops do not enjoy any immunities.

The matter of legal immunities for MFO personnel was the object of considerable disagreement between the parties. The US originally wanted the MFO to enjoy the same immunities and benefits as those accorded to UNEF-I. The basis of the problem was that Israeli legal and security officials wished to retain extensive powers of arrest and prosecution over the MFO members in cases of alleged serious criminal offenses. In particular, Israel wished to have legal authority in cases of suspected arms smuggling, especially in view of a 1979 incident in which a UN officer was convicted in Israel for gun running for the PLO in Lebanon. Israel eventually agreed to soften its position on this subject, as top policy makers felt that their reservations were outweighed by political considerations.

On behalf of the States participating in the MFO, the US pressed Israel to withdraw or soften its demands for legal jurisdiction over MFO personnel in criminal cases. It was understood that Prime Minister Begin had taken part in top-level consultations on this issue. As the date for the deployment of the MFO in the Sinai approached, the basic policy appeared to be to avoid, or at least narrow, any dispute with the participating States.[1] Israel nevertheless insisted, and the MFO decided, that until an agreement was reached with the MFO participant governments, members of the Force would not be permitted to enter Israel to spend their vacations.[2]

The attitude of the US was that Israel should hardly be concerned over immunities of MFO members, as the Force would be stationed entirely on the Egyptian side of the border, in the Sinai. Why, then, should Israel fight Egypt's battle as regards immunities? In a letter dated March 15, 1982, the MFO Director-General, to facilitate his negotiations with participating States, asked Egypt and Israel to confirm that the members of the MFO "shall have the rights, duties, privileges and immunities in accordance with the Protocol." Israel confirmed this on the same day. Ultimately, the US view prevailed. Israel has entered into supplementary agreements (in accordance with Article 11 (d) of the Appendix to the Protocol) with nine of the participating States setting out the immunities granted to members on leave in Israel (see below). The Israeli domestic legislation in this regard is discussed below.

The privileges and immunities extended to the MFO are based on the model of the 1957 Egypt-UN agreement on UNEF-I, which granted extensive immunities to the Force.[3] The MFO Protocol provides that each party shall accord the MFO the privileges and immunities indicated in the Appendix, which include the following:[4]

THE DIRECTOR-GENERAL

According to the MFO Protocol, .
The Director-General, his deputy, the Commander, and his

> deputy, shall be accorded in respect of themselves, their spouses and minor children, the privileges and immunities, exemptions and facilities accorded to diplomatic envoys in accordance with international law.[5]

In effect, the privileges and immunities of these persons are governed by the 1961 Vienna Convention on Diplomatic Relations.[6] Israel has granted the Director-General diplomatic immunity.

THE FORCE

As for the privileges and immunities of the Force as a unit, the MFO may display its special flag or insignia on its headquarters, camps, posts, or other premises, vehicles, boats, etc.[7] MFO vehicles, boats and aircraft are not subject to registration and licensing under the laws and regulations of the Receiving State. Moreover, the authorities of the Receiving State must accept as valid, without a test or fee, a permit or license for operating service vehicles, boats and aircraft issued by the Director-General.[8]

MFO premises are inviolable. Without prejudice to the fact that all the premises of the MFO remain in the territory of the Receiving State, they are subject to the exclusive control and authority of the Director-General, who alone may consent to the entry of officials to perform duties on such premises.[9]

The MFO enjoys the status, privileges and immunities accorded in Article 2 of the Convention on the Privileges and Immunities of the United Nations which regulates privileges and immunities as regards property, funds and assets. The property, funds and assets of the Participating State used in the Receiving State in connection with MFO activities enjoy immunity from every form of legal process, unless waived in a particular case. Waiver of immunity does not, however, extend to any measure of execution (Convention, Sec. 2). The archives and documents of the Force are inviolable. The property and assets of the Force enjoy immunity from search, requisition, confiscation, expropriation and any other form of interference, whether by executive, administrative, judicial or legislative action (Secs. 3, 4). The Force may hold funds, gold or any currency without restrictions, and may transfer these between countries or convert them to other currencies (Sec. 5). The Force, its assets, income and property are exempt from all direct taxes (other than charges for public utility services), as well as from customs duties and import or export restrictions on items for official use (the latter may not be resold in the Receiving State without the Government's permission) (Sec. 7). These provisions also apply to the property, funds and assets of Participating States used in the Receiving State in connection with the activities of the MFO.[10]

These provisions closely follow the UNEF-I Regulations. According to the latter, UNEF, as a subsidiary UN organ, enjoyed the status, privileges and immunities of the Organization as established by the Convention on the Privileges and Immunities of the United Nations. In this way, the independent exercise of the functions of UNEF was ensured as regards property supplied by the UN. It was necessary, however, to make provision for supplies and equipment belonging to national contingents. It was therefore stipulated that the relevant terms of the Convention would also apply to the property, funds and assets of the Participating States used in the Host State in connection with service in the Force. (The entry without duty of equipment and supplies of the Force, and of personal effects of members of the Force upon their first arrival, was to be arranged with the individual Host State.)[11]

Freedom of Movement

The MFO's access across the international boundary is permitted only through entry checkpoints designated by each party. Such access must be according to the laws and regulations of each State. Each party must establish adequate procedures to facilitate such entries.[12] Within the respective Zones, MFO troops enjoy freedom of movement necessary for the performance of their tasks.[13]

When the MFO uses roads, bridges, port facilities and

airfields, it is not subject to payment of registration or other dues, tolls or charges, in the areas where it functions and the normal points of access (except for charges directly related to services rendered).[14]   It has been pointed out that the effectiveness of the Force will depend on its freedom of movement. It would be easy to impede the proper functioning of the Force through various bureaucratic and technical limitations, such as failing to provide a liaison officer to accompany a given unit, or requiring prior notification for every movement by the Force. Israel made it clear that the Force should not be subject to any limitations in Zone C. The only exceptions are the coordination of MFO movements in civilian installations with Egyptian civilian police, and routine coordination of MFO flights with civilian flight control.[15]

Freedom of Communication

The Director-General has the authority to install and operate communications systems as necessary for the performance of the MFO's functions.[16]

The MFO enjoys the facilities in respect to communications provided for in the Convention on the Privileges and Immunities of the United Nations. Article 3 of the latter stipulates that the Force "shall enjoy in the territory of each Member for its official communications treatment not less favourable than that accorded by the Government of that Member to any other Government, including its diplomatic mission, in the matter of priorities, rates and taxes on mails, cables, telegrams, radiograms, telephotos, telephone and other communications; and press rates for information to the press and radio." No censorship may be applied to its official correspondence and communications. The Force has the right to use codes and to dispatch and receive its correspondence by courier or in bags, which enjoy the same immunities as diplomatic couriers and bags.[17]

Likewise, in the areas where it functions, the MFO enjoys the right to unrestricted communication by radio, telephone, telegraph or any other means, and of establishing the necessary facilities for maintaining such communications within and between premises of the MFO, including the laying of cables and land lines and the establishment of fixed and mobile radio sending and receiving stations.[18]

MEMBERS OF THE FORCE

Jurisdiction

It is considered essential for the preservation of the independent exercise of the functions of a multinational force that its members be immune from the criminal jurisdiction of the host State. Moreover, such a policy facilitates the decision of the contributing States to send troops to the Force.

On the other hand, it is crucial that the waiving of jurisdiction by the host State should not create a jurisdictional vacuum, wherein an offense committed might not be subject to prosecution either by the host State or the contributing State. Adequate provisions to prevent this must be ensured.

Under any circumstance, it is understood that any arrangements made respecting criminal and civil jurisdiction are to take into account the special functions of the Force, and are not for the personal benefit of the members of the Force.[19]

a. Criminal Jurisdiction

MFO members enjoy complete immunity from criminal jurisdiction, but the Sending State in question is duty-bound to prosecute its nationals in accordance with its laws.

Criminal Jurisdiction

11. (a) Military members of the MFO and members of the civilian observer group of the MFO shall be subject to the exclusive jurisdiction of their respective national states in respect of any criminal offenses which may be committed by them in the Receiving State. Any such person who is

> charged with the commission of a crime will be brought to trial by the respective Participating State, in accordance with its laws.
> (b) Subject to paragraph 25, other members of the MFO shall be immune from the criminal jurisdiction of the Receiving State [only] in respect of words spoken or written and all acts performed by them in their official capacity.

In other words, non-military members of the MFO enjoy functional immunity from criminal jurisdiction. Residents of the Receiving State who work for the MFO do not enjoy any immunity. In order to mitigate the absolute immunity of military MFO members from criminal jurisdiction,

> (c) [1] The Director-General shall obtain the assurances of each Participating State that it will be prepared to take the necessary measures to assure proper discipline of its personnel and to exercise jurisdiction with respect to any crime or offense which might be committed by its personnel. The Director-General shall comply with requests of the Receiving State for the withdrawal from its territory of any member of the MFO who violates its laws, regulations, customs or traditions.
> [2] The Director-General, with the consent of the Participating State, may waive the immunity of a member of the MFO [or of a given category of soldiers].
> (d) Without prejudice to the foregoing, a Participating State may enter into a supplementary arrangement with the Receiving State to limit or waive the immunities of its members of the MFO who are on periods of leave while in the Receiving State.[20]

The immunity from criminal jurisdiction applies to MFO members not only in regard to their official capacity, but also when they are on vacation. However, the Receiving State has the option, as stated in paragraph (d) above, of entering into additional agreements with any Sending State for the latter to curtail or renounce the immunities of its troops while on vacation in the receiving territory.

Israel availed herself of the opportunity to enter into supplementary agreements with individual participating States to limit or waive the immunities of their members of the MFO who are on leave on Israeli territory. Negotiations took place regarding the conclusion of such additional agreements, and until their implementation, the immunities held. As a practical matter, MFO troops are not stationed on Israeli soil, and Israel had the option of refusing admittance to vacationing MFO personnel from any country which had not yet concluded such an agreement. Each agreement on immunities and privileges was negotiated between Israel and the interested Participating State. Most of the negotiations took place in Washington for logistic reasons, because the Israeli Ambassador to the US and his colleagues from the various Participating States were in charge of the negotiations.

As stated, agreements regarding immunities of troops on Israeli soil have been signed between Israel and nine of the ten participants (excluding France).[21] They provide that while on leave in Israel, military personnel and civilian observers enjoy immunity from Israeli criminal jurisdiction, except in regard to certain offenses involving drugs, weapons and explosives.[22] Assurances were given, however, that any charge sheet would be approved by the Attorney-General. As for possession of dangerous drugs for personal use and other offenses, the immunity holds only for judicial proceedings, but not for conducting an investigation. Detention for the latter purpose for a period of more than seven days also is subject to the approval of the Attorney-General.[23]

b. Civil Jurisdiction

As for civil jurisdiction, immunity is granted to MFO members only with respect to their official duties (functional immunity).

> 12. Members of the MFO shall not be subject to the civil jurisdiction of the courts of the Receiving State or to other legal process in any matter relating to their official duties. ... If the Director-General certifies that a member of the MFO is unable because of official duties or authorized absence to protect his interests in a civil proceeding in which he is a participant, the court or authority shall at his request suspend the proceeding until the elimination of the disability, but for not more than

> ninety days. Property of a member of the
> MFO which is certified by the
> Director-General to be needed by him for
> the fulfillment of his official duties shall
> be free from seizure for the satisfaction of
> a judgment, decision or order, together with
> other property not subject thereto under the
> law of the Receiving State. The personal
> liberty of a member of the MFO shall not be
> restricted by a court or other authority of
> the Receiving State in a civil proceeding,
> whether to enforce a judgment, decision or
> order, to compel an oath of disclosure, or
> for any other reason.
> ...

Notification: Certification

> 13.   ... The Director-General [is empowered to]
> certify to the court whether or not the
> [civil] proceeding is related to the
> official duties of such member.[24]

c.   Jurisdiction over UNEF-I: A Comparison

For purposes of comparison, it is interesting to examine the provisions for jurisdiction over UNEF-I, the model on which MFO immunities are based. The UNEF Regulations provided that members of the Force were subject to the criminal jurisdiction of their respective national States, and not to the criminal jurisdiction of the courts of the host State. Responsibility for the exercise of criminal jurisdiction rested with the authorities of the sending State, including, as appropriate, the commanders of the national contingents.[25] The Agreement with Egypt provided that members of the Force should be under the exclusive jurisdiction of their respective national States with regard to any criminal offenses committed by them in Egypt.[26]

As regards civil jurisdiction, members of UNEF were not subject to the jurisdiction of the courts of the host State or to other legal processes in any matter relating to their official duties.[27] While members of UNEF enjoyed functional immunity from civil jurisdiction, the same machinery was available for settlement as for any claims against the UN. In other civil cases, where jurisdiction over a member of the Force might be exercised by

Egypt, there were agreed upon measures to prevent the proceedings from interfering with the performance of official duties.[28]

The agreements between the UN and the participating States specified that this "immunity from the jurisdiction of Egypt is based on the understanding that the authorities of the participating States would exercise such jurisdiction as might be necessary with respect to crimes or offences committed in Egypt by any members of the Force provided from their own military services." Consequently, the UN Secretary-General sought assurance from each participating Government that it would be prepared to exercise its jurisdiction over any crime or offenses that might be committed by a member of its contingent.

This legal arrangement was subject to potential conflict, given the varied legal systems and terms of military law in participating States. For example, national laws differ regarding the extent to which they confer martial jurisdiction on courts over civil offenses in peacetime, or confer on either military or civil courts jurisdiction over offenses committed abroad. Some stipulate that a trial can only take place in the home country, and this raises practical questions about the submission of evidence.[29]

Given the potentially adverse impact of criminal offenses perpetrated by members of multinational forces and the trend to grant the personnel of international forces -- whether or not under UN auspices -- immunity from the criminal jurisdiction of the host State, it is important that the legal systems of the contributing States function adequately to prevent and punish criminal conduct of their personnel. "Community policy considerations involved here are not only those favoring IMF [International Military Forces] effectiveness in achieving its objectives, but also fundamental perspectives of human dignity, requiring the protection of human life and well-being, respect, wealth and other values."

Recommendations toward this end include the promotion of the exercise of contributing State jurisdiction over serious military offenses; the improvement of the judicial competence of contributing States through domestic legislative modifications; and the promotion of eventual international competence through comparative legal research and of draft proposals. Moreover, since "criminal offenses by a member of one national contingent against a member of another contingent, or against inhabitants of the host state, obviously have substantial adverse impact on interests other than those of the intergovernmental organization sponsoring the IMF and the state of whose military forces the accused is a member," it is felt that "Recommendations for the allocating of criminal jurisdiction between contributing states or between the contributing state and the host state might call for less deference to the exclusive interests of the contributing state of whose military forces the accused is a member."[30]

Exemption from Taxation, Customs and Fiscal Regulations

Members of the MFO are exempt from taxation by the Receiving State on the pay and emoluments received from their national governments or from the MFO. They are also exempt from all other direct taxes, fees and charges, except for those levied for services rendered.[31]

MFO members also have the right to import free of duty their personal effects in connection with their first taking up their post in the Receiving State. Regarding personal property not required by them by reason of their serving with the MFO in the Receiving State, they shall be subject to the laws and regulations of the Receiving State governing customs and foreign exchange.[32]

Provisions are made for the exemption from customs and import duty fees. The Government of the Receiving State recognizes the right of the MFO to import free of duty equipment and provisions, supplies and other goods for the exclusive use of members of the MFO, including the right of the MFO to establish, maintain and operate at headquarters, camps and posts, service institutes providing amenities for the members of the MFO.[33] The Director-General is to take all necessary measures to prevent any abuse of the exemption and to prevent the sale or resale of such goods to persons other than the members of the MFO. Sympathetic consideration is to be given by the Director-General to observations or requests of the authorities of the Receiving State concerning the operation of service institutes.

Indeed, much of the effective functioning of the administration of justice in regard to the MFO seems to depend on the role of the Director-General and his interpretation of it.

> The Director-General shall cooperate at all times with the appropriate authorities of the Receiving State to facilitate the proper administration of justice, secure the observance of laws and regulations and prevent the occurrence of any abuse in connection with the privileges, immunities and facilities mentioned in this Appendix.
> ...The Director-General will take the measures within his power with respect to crimes or offenses committed against citizens of the Receiving State by members of the MFO.[34]

The _Knesset_ approved the Protocol and accompanying documents on July 27, 1981. The Israeli legislative framework for the MFO's immunities in accordance with the Protocol is the Immunities and Privileges (Multilateral Force) Law, 1982, passed by the _Knesset_ on January 26, 1982.[35] The special law was promulgated because the Status of International Organizations Law, 1980, does not seem to cover the MFO. The existing Israeli law only granted immunities to a permanent mission and its staff, and in the case of the MFO the permanent headquarters are in Rome. The contemplated immunities for the MFO applied to soldiers who are not in Israel on a permanent basis, and the scope of the existing law was inappropriate in that it granted overly wide immunities.

The 1982 Law empowers the Minister for Foreign Affairs and the Minister of Justice to determine those immunities and privileges to be accorded to the MFO and its members. (As a temporary measure they were likewise entitled to grant such privileges and immunities to persons and bodies setting up the MFO, for a period of one year or less.) Orders granting exemptions from taxes or from other mandatory payments require the approval of the Minister of

Finance. Orders granting privileges and immunities must have the approval of a joint committee of the Constitution, Legislation and Juridical Committee and the Foreign Affairs and Security Committee of the <u>Knesset</u>. The Minister for Foreign Affairs is responsible for the implementation of the Law.

In accordance with the 1982 Law, the Ministers for Foreign Affairs and of Justice issued the Immunities and Privileges (MFO) Order, 1983, which grants privileges and immunities in accordance with the Protocol and also gives expression to the supplementary arrangements with the contributing States. It provides that

[1] the MFO and its personnel shall enjoy all the immunities and privileges permitted according to the Law.

[2] these immunities and privileges shall not apply, however, to MFO members who are not on duty

(1) as regards offences under Section 144 of the Penal Law, 1977 (concerning unlawful possession of weapons) and under Sections 7, and 13 to 20 of the Dangerous Drugs Ordinance [New Version], 1973 (concerning possession and use, trade and traffic), except for an offence of possessing or using a dangerous drug for the sole use of the possessor or user according to Section 7 of the Ordinance, and including offences of attempting, persuading and conspiring to commit one of the above offences;

(2) as regards suspicion of a crime or offence of possessing a dangerous drug or its use solely by the possessor or of the user according to Section 7 of the Ordinance -- as concerns arrest, search or interrogation.

(3) The following may not be issued without the approval of the Attorney-General --

(1) a charge sheet for an offence according to Section 2 (1);

(2) a request to a court to detain a suspect under Section 2 (2) for a period of more than seven days from the beginning of the detention.[36]

As far as can be ascertained it would appear that Egypt did not promulgate any internal measures regarding the privileges and immunities of the MFO on its territory. Therefore the provisions in the MFO Protocol hold, and the MFO enjoys all the immunities therein.

100

NOTES

(1) David Landau, "Israel Prepared to Soften Stand on MFO Immunities," Jerusalem Post, March 12, 1982, p. 2.
(2) David Landau, Yedi'ot Aharonot, March 21, 1982, p. 8.
(3) This agreement was effected by exchange of letters on February 8, 1957, between the Secretary-General on behalf of the UN, and the Minister for Foreign Affairs of Egypt. It was approved by the General Assembly in Res. 1121 (XI), Feb. 22, 1957. Text in UN Doc. A/3526, GAOR, 11th Sess., Annexes, a.i. 66, at 52 ff. See Gabriella Rosner, The United Nations Emergency Force 142-45 (N.Y. 1963).
(4) MFO Annex, Art. 33.
(5) MFO Appendix, Art. 25.
(6) 500 U.N.T.S. 95, esp. Arts. 29-37; 55 Am. J. Intl. L. 1062 (1961).
(7) See MFO Annex, Art. 20 for details.
(8) Ibid., Art. 21.
(9) MFO Appendix, Art. 19.
(10) Ibid., Art. 23. Convention 1 U.N.T.S. 15.
(11) Regulation 10, "Regulations for the United Nations Emergency Force," Feb. 20, 1957 (UN Doc. ST/SGB/UNEF/1); text in Rosalyn Higgins, United Nations Peacekeeping 1946-1967 -- Documents and Commentary, Vol. I: The Middle East 288 (London 1969) (hereinafter: Higgins); Elihu Lauterpacht, The United Nations Emergency Force: Basic Documents 34, at 37 (London 1960).
(12) MFO Annex, Art. 4.
(13) Ibid., Art. 14.
(14) MFO Appendix, Art. 33.
(15) "The Multinational Force" (Hebrew), Ma'arachot (No. 283) 30 (July 1982).
(16) MFO Appendix, Art. 29. This is subject to the provisions of Art. 35 of the [Torremolinos] International Telecommunications Convention of April 11, 1973, relating to harmful interference. This Convention is no longer in force. The provision appears in the [Nairobi] International Telecommunications Convention of 1982. Art. 35 has remained unchanged, only with paragraphs 135-136 renumbered as 158-159:

ARTICLE 35
Harmful Interference

158 1. "All stations, whatever their purpose, must be established and operated in such a manner as not to cause harmful interference to the radio services or communications of other Members or of recognized private operating agencies, or of other duly authorized operating agencies which carry on radio service, and which operate in accordance with the provisions of the Radio Regulations.

159 2. Each Member undertakes to require the private operating agencies which it recognizes and the other operating agencies duly authorized for this purpose, to observe the provisions of 158."

On the domestic plane, the provision is in force in Israel.

(17) 1 U.N.T.S. 15, Secs. 9 & 10.

(18) MFO Appendix, Art. 30.   For MFO rights regarding water, electricity and other public utilities, see ibid., Art. 34.

(19) See Exchange of Letters constituting an Agreement between the United Nations and the Government of Egypt concerning the Status of the United Nations Emergency Force in Egypt, para. 10 (text in Lauterpacht, supra note 11, at 20).

(20) MFO Appendix, Art. 11.

(21) France was apparently unwilling to sign an immunities agreement that includes a clause referring to Israel and all its territories.   France considered this a devious way for Israel to seek recognition of its status in the territories. (Interview with a European official.)

(22) MFO Annual Report, 1983, p. 11. The agreement between the US and Israel in this regard was effected by an exchange of notes of September 28 and October 1, 1982.   The agreements with the other participant States were effected in the same manner.

(23) Lapidoth, p. 384.

(24) MFO Appendix, Arts. 12, 13.

(25) Regulation 34 (a), supra note 11.

(26) Para. 11, supra note 19.

(27) Regulation 34 (b), supra note 11.   Agreement, supra note 19, para. 12.

(28) Agreement, supra note 19, paras. 12 & 38(b). See Higgins, at 509, para. 138.

(29) Summary Study of the Experience derived from the Establishment and Operation of the Force: Report of the Secretary-General, Oct. 9, 1958 (UN Doc. A/3943); text in Higgins, p. 483, at 509, paras. 136-37.

(30) Walter L. Williams, Jr., Intergovernmental Military Forces and World Public Order 621-22 (Leiden 1971).

(31) MFO Appendix, Art. 26.

(32) Ibid., Art. 27. For the role of the Director-General in this regard, see Arts. 27, 28.

(33)"The amenities that may be provided by service institutes shall be goods of a consumable nature (tobacco and tobacco products, beer, etc.), and other customary articles of small value. To the end that duty-free importation for the MFO may be effected with the least possible delay, having regard to the interests of the government of the Receiving State, a mutually satisfactory procedure, including documentation, shall be arranged between the Director-General and the customs authorities of the Receiving State." Ibid., Art. 23.

(34) Ibid., Arts. 10, 18.   On the Director-General, see also Arts. 12 (b), 14, 17, 18.

(35) Sefer Hahukim (Statutes of the State of Israel) (No. 1039), Feb. 3, 1982, p. 30. For Bill see Hatza'ot Hok (Legislative Bills of the State of Israel) (No. 1552), Oct. 29, 1981. (Status of International Organizations Law, in Sefer Hahukim (No. 978), July 31, 1980, p. 163).

(36) Kovetz Hatakanot (Regulations of the State of Israel) (No. 4455), Jan. 25, 1983, pp. 683-84. This is in accordance with the Exchange of Notes, supra at note 22.

7
Settlement of Disputes

The MFO Protocol stipulates in Article 8 that disputes arising from its interpretation and application shall be resolved in accordance with the procedure set forth in Article 7 of the Peace Treaty. The latter provides that such disputes shall be resolved by negotiations. Should this method fail, disputes shall be resolved by conciliation or submitted to arbitration.[1] This provision seems to apply only to disputes between the parties and not to those between one of the parties and the MFO.[2] As pointed out by Theodor Meron, Article 7 of the Peace Treaty -- and by analogy Article 8 of the Protocol -- "does not impose on either party any substantive legal obligations except ... to act in good faith."[3] This provision is thus not directly applicable, and merely provides the general framework. An additional agreement would be required for each specific dispute. Various questions are left open by these provisions: At what stage should negotiation be abandoned in favor of conciliation or arbitration? Do one or both of the parties have to request conciliation or arbitration? Who will be the members of the conciliation commission or the arbitration board, and according to which rules will the arbitrators work? Thus in order to implement these provisions on the settlement of disputes in any given case an additional agreement would be necessary.[4]

A different provision applies to disputes between one of the host countries and the MFO. Disputes concerning the interpretation or application of the Appendix of the MFO Protocol (dealing with the duties, privileges and immunities of the MFO) which are not resolved by negotiation or another agreed upon mode of settlement are to be referred for final settlement to a tribunal of three arbitrators.[5] Disputes concerning the terms of employment and conditions of service of locally recruited personnel shall be settled by administrative procedures to be established by the Director-General.[6]

Disputes or claims of a private law character are to be settled by a claims commission established for that purpose. This includes any claim made by (1) a resident of the Receiving State (Egypt or Israel) against the MFO or a member thereof, in respect of any damages alleged to result from an act or omission of such member of the MFO relating to his official duties; (2) the Government of Egypt or Israel against a member of the MFO; (3) the MFO or the Government of the Receiving State against one another (unless it involves the interpretation or application of the Appendix to the Protocol).[7]

With respect to the first of these, i.e. cases of civil jurisdiction arising from a matter relating to official duties and which involves a member of the MFO and a resident of the Receiving State, there may be problems of implementation that may lead to absurd results. Under UNEF the procedure was relatively simple. Persons would bring their claims before the UN Secretary-General, and claims commissions were never established. In the case of the MFO, there might be instances in which there would be two claims commissions and the transmission of the claim would be without verification. It is not certain that the transfer of claims is well provided for, and it may be speculated that if claims commissions are ever established under this framework, there might be problems of lack of coordination in their implementation.[8]

As for other disputes or claims to which the MFO is a party arising out of contract or otherwise of a private law character, the MFO shall make provisions for the appropriate modes of settlement. In the event that no such provisions have been made with the contracting party, such claims are to be settled by a claims commission established for that purpose.[9]

It was understood that in practice, wherever possible, the MFO Director-General and the Commander would seek to resolve disputes through contact with working-level Israeli and Egyptian officials, in order to avoid political consequences.

NOTES

(1) MFO Protocol, Art. 8; Peace Treaty, Art. 7.
(2) Lapidoth, p. 379.
(3) See Theodor Meron, "Settlement of Disputes and the Treaty of Peace: The Israel Perspective", 15 Is. L. Rev. 269, 273 (1980).
(4) Lapidoth, p. 379.
(5) MFO Appendix, Arts. 40, 41.
One arbitrator is to be named by the Director-General, one by the Governmnent of the Receiving State, and an umpire to be chosen jointly shall preside over the proceedings. If the two parties fail to agree on the appointment of the umpire within one month of the proposal of arbitration by one of the parties, the two members selected by them shall select a chairman from the list of the Permanent Court of Arbitration. Two members of the tribunal shall constitute a quorum for the performance of its functions, and for all deliberations and decisions of the tribunal a favorable vote of two members shall be sufficient.
(6) MFO Appendix, Art. 39.
(7) MFO Appendix, Art. 38 (b).
The Commission shall consist of one member appointed by the Director-General, one member by the Government of the Receiving State (Egypt or Israel as the case may be) and a Chairman jointly appointed by the two. If there is no agreement on the Chairman, the first two members selected shall select one from the list of the Permanent Court of Arbitration.
(8) According to UNEF Regulations (34(d))
"Disputes involving the Force and its members shall be settled in accordance with such procedures provided by the Secretary-General as may be required, including the establishment of a claims commission or commissions. Supplemental instructions defining the jurisdiction of such commissions or other bodies as may be established shall be issued by the Secretary-General..."
(In Higgins, p. 292).
(9) MFO Appendix, Art. 38 (a).

8
Withdrawal

Israel learned a bitter lesson when Egypt's request for the withdrawal of UNEF-I from the Sinai in 1967 met with the prompt approval of the UN Secretary-General. This was followed by the June 1967 War.[1] Israel therefore insisted early on that the UN Force to be established under the Egypt-Israel Peace Treaty not be withdrawn without the consent of the two parties, or by the positive vote of the five permanent members of the Security Council. Indeed, the Peace Treaty provides that

> The Parties agree not to request withdrawal of the United Nations personnel and that these personnel will not be removed unless such removal is approved by the Security Council of the United Nations, with the affirmative vote of the five Permanent Members, unless the Parties otherwise agree (Article 4 (2)).

According to the MFO Protocol (Article 3), this provision may be reviewed and amended by mutual agreement of both parties. From this it is clear that withdrawal may be effected only by mutual consent of both parties.

A crucial problem regarding the MFO is who in fact is "in charge" of the Force, and therefore in a position to order its withdrawal. For UN forces the UN Secretary-General in effect serves as the civilian commander. The authority for withdrawing the Force, had it been under UN auspices, would have been the UN Security Council, based in this case on the consent of all of its five permanent members. In the case of the MFO, it was agreed that the power of withdrawal would rest with the parties.

The question of the withdrawal of the MFO is distinct from the case of individual contingents withdrawing from the Force (although it may be theoretically envisioned that the removal of most of the contingents from the MFO would force the withdrawal of the MFO itself). According to the MFO Protocol, the Director-General is to impress on the contributing nations "the importance of continuity of service in units with the MFO so that the Commander may be in a position to plan his operations with knowledge of what units will be available. The Director-General shall obtain the agreement of contributing nations that the national contingents shall not be withdrawn without adequate prior notification to the Director-General."[2]

The US made a commitment to "use its best efforts to find acceptable replacements for contingents that withdraw from the MFO." More generally, the US expressed its readiness "to take those steps necessary to ensure the maintenance of an acceptable MFO." US domestic legislation provides that if a country withdraws from the MFO with the result that the military personnel of less than four foreign countries remain, the US must make every possible effort "to find promptly a country to replace that country."[3]

Though the Protocol stipulates that a State wishing to withdraw its contingent from the MFO must give the Director-General sufficient notice, the period of time for prior notification is not indicated. According to Mr. Hunt, the first Director-General, it is generally agreed that the MFO would require a minimum of six months notice. The MFO does not maintain a list of alternate countries willing to participate in case of withdrawal by current participants.[4]

The problems created by States withdrawing their contingents lie not only in soliciting alternative States willing to contribute, but also in locating States that are able to do so. As pointed out by the Director-General, the number of countries that are able to provide helicopters, fixed wing airplanes and ships, and communications equipment and knowhow, is relatively limited.

The current personnel is highly trained and the contributing State must provide the expensive equipment necessary. A limited number of States are able to do so.[5]

NOTES

(1) See Higgins, pp. 219 ff. Jack Israel Garvey, "United Nations Peacekeeping and Host State Consent," 64 Am. J. Int'l L. 241 (1970). Indar Jit Rikhye, The Sinai Blunder (London 1980).

(2) MFO Annex, Art. 3. See MFO House Hearings, pp. 14-16, 27-28.

(3) Identical letter from Alexander Haig to Egypt and Israel, Aug. 3, 1981, paras. 3 (C & D). 20 Int'l Legal Materials (No. 5) 1190 (Sept. 1981); 26 Kitvei Amana (No. 896), 663, at 664. P.L. 97-132, Sec. 3 (a)(2)(B).

(4) Hunt Press Conference, Jan. 17, 1983, p. 10. (See supra, Ch. 3, section on "Alternatives.")

(5) Hunt Press Conference, Jan. 17, 1983, p. 10.

9
Conclusion

The MFO is the first effective large-scale multinational peacekeeping operation (the Arab force in Lebanon not qualifying as such) set up independently of the framework of the UN or another international organization such as the OAS or the Arab League. As such, it presents an alternative for maintaining security in those areas or situations where the power politics in the UN effectively prevent UN participation in maintaining the peace.

There are several structural differences between the MFO and conventional UN forces:[1]

1.   The existence of the MFO is not dependent on the international organ establishing it (e.g. the UN General Assembly, as in the case of UNEF-I in the Sinai, or the UN Security Council in the case of UNEF-II). The legal validity of the MFO stems from the agreement of Egypt and Israel, as set forth in the MFO Protocol. ("A Multinational Force and Observers is hereby established ..."; Art. 1.)

2.   The MFO had to work out a fresh structure for itself, as it is not connected with existing headquarters of an international organization. All regulations for the functioning of the Force had to be established to conform with the special circumstances of the MFO. The disadvantage is that initially the lack of an established administrative and political structure created some difficulties, but in the long run the new structure "held the promise of finding better ways in an environment relatively free of the accumulated

bureaucratic   weight and political complexity of an existing
organization."[2]

At the same time, it would be an over-simplification to
maintain that a non-UN force is ipso facto superior to a force
under UN auspices.   Even outside the framework of the UN, it may be
asked to what extent the MFO is an original creation, and to what
extent it mirrors the structure and organization of the UN,
including the problems the latter entails, for there is a natural
gravitation towards the UN model.

3.   The financing of the MFO is not dependent on outside factors
in the form of States opposed to its functioning, as Egypt, Israel
and the US share equally in the entire financial burden of
supporting the Force.   It has been pointed out that this
arrangement emphasizes the direct responsibility of the three
parties involved in the maintenance of the Force.   "The fact of
Egyptian and Israeli financial participation could be expected to
produce a healthy sense of identification with the organization,
but at the same time created an obligation for the negotiators to
devise methods of ensuring objectivity and independence."[3]   Any
default in payment would impede the functioning of the Force within
a short time.

In this sense, in case of default of payment by one of the
parties (a violation of the Protocol), it would perhaps be more
difficult to maintain the Force than in the case of a UN force,
which continues to be financed by the Organization even in case of
payment arrears by an individual member State.   In the case of the
MFO, the US would no doubt be called upon to take up the debt of
the violating party.   This in turn leads to the question of who in
practice holds the key to maintaining the MFO -- Egypt and Israel,
or the US.

4.   The role of the US in the Force -- in terms of commitments,
support, contributions and financing -- is far greater than the
role of any single State in a UN force.   In fact, the US role in
the MFO is reminiscent in some ways of the US position in the
unique US-led force in Korea.   Since the US enjoys prestige and

influence with both Egypt and Israel, the chances of success for
the MFO are increased. Moreover, the US provided relatively easy
access to an existing logistic system and to expertise resulting
from the Sinai Field Mission experience.

5. The absence of UN backing renders the MFO unacceptable to
certain political camps, and initially it was feared by the US,
Egypt and Israel that the MFO would not be accepted internationally
as a legitimate peacekeeping force capable of attracting a "broadly
based" group of participating States.[4]

On the other hand, being independent of the UN, the MFO is not
subject to the requirement that the Force be composed of
contingents representing "equitable geographic distribution," as is
the case with UN forces. The MFO does not rely on the support of
the Arab-Soviet and Non-Aligned anti-Israel majority which
determines UN policies. In UN forces there were contingents
hostile to Israel. The MFO, on the other hand, is comprised of
contingents from States maintaining diplomatic relations with both
Israel and Egypt and who are acceptable to both countries.

6. The MFO was designed to be durable. Its mandate is not
subject to periodic review and renewal.[5] The uncertainty and
debate over renewal of UN forces such as UNEF every six months is a
source of tension and uncertainty.

7. As stated, withdrawal of the MFO may only occur with the
approval of both Egypt and Israel (Protocol, Art. 3), and does not
depend on an outside body like the UN. This is unlike the
situation in 1967 when UNEF-I withdrew upon Egypt's request alone.

Despite these advantages offered by the MFO over a UN force,
the MFO itself cannot guarantee the Peace Treaty. On the contrary,
the Peace Treaty is a prerequisite for the Force. Only if the
Peace Treaty stands can the MFO fulfill its function properly. As
events in Lebanon have tragically shown, a multinational force of
this kind, designed for peacekeeping, is impotent at the task of
peace-making.[6]

The flexibility that permitted the change from a UN force as
originally envisaged to a ten-nation self-organized force, and the

open-mindedness of the three parties involved in the negotiations in agreeing to change certain operative provisions of the Peace Treaty in order to comply with the broader aim of that Treaty is commendable.[7] Such adaptability ought to be displayed in other international dealings.

UN forces have been criticized for a variety of faults. It is useful to analyze some of these deficiencies in order to evaluate the prospects for non-UN peacekeeping.

> The problems faced by UN units over the years include impaired military efficiency because of the political requirement of representative heterogeneity in composition; inadequate security because of the emphasis upon negotiation and a restrictive interpretation of self-defence; dangers of involvement in domestic power struggles when confronted with an authority vacuum in the host country; financial hiccups; non-cooperation from major powers or local belligerents; reluctance on the part of lesser powers to contribute contingents; and erosion of credibility as conflicts appear no nearer to political solution after years of peacekeeping.[8]

Some of the problems of recent UN forces have been discussed in a report by Roger A. Brooks for the Heritage Foundation.[9] The Soviet Union has rendered UN peacekeeping impotent by the frequent threat or use of the veto to paralyze the Security Council. The USSR is in arrears for payments for peacekeeping operations for about $119.3 million (the US has contributed more than $1 billion, or one-third of the total UN peacekeeping bill).

As regards UNIFIL, the Report notes the uneven ability of its forces to assert the necessary authority. Thus, while some units acted boldly against PLO contingents in Lebanon moving through the area under their control, elsewhere there were weak spots in the UNIFIL line through which the PLO was able to maneuver. As pointed out by the Report, it requires well-trained soldiers to deter conflict. Two further problems that UNIFIL shares with earlier UN forces are lack of familiarity with the terrain and inadequate intelligence operations. Moreover, the inability of the UN to ensure "freedom of movement" has been a continuing problem for UNIFIL. UNIFIL has also been accused of partiality.[10] Some of

these problems are undoubtedly due to the complex nature of
Lebanon's political makeup which would render the task of any force
extremely difficult. The "multinational force" (MNF) operating in
Lebanon was not comparable to the MFO in that it lacked an overall
structure and was rather constituted of several separate
contingents.

Professor Ruth Lapidoth has pointed out that in terms of
political influence and effectiveness the MFO may be preferable to
any force the UN might have established. This is because a force
sponsored by the Security Council is subject to decisions based
mainly on political considerations and the competing influences of
the superpowers. The composition and operating procedures of a UN
force would have been determined by the UN Secretary-General based
on criteria that are alien to the Middle East and the Peace Treaty.
On the other hand, the political considerations upon which the
formation of the MFO was based have removed it from the East-West
tensions prevalent at the UN and increase the confidence of all the
parties involved in its success.[11]

Nevertheless, in some circles there remains a preference for a
UN force. Egypt maintained UNTSO on its soil on the basis of its
own sovereignty, but the latter has no security function to
fulfill. Egypt keeps UNTSO in order to have the option of
returning to a UN force. In 1982 Israel communicated to Egypt
through diplomatic channels that UNTSO did not fulfill any function
in Sinai. As stated by Butros Ghali, UNTSO or another UN force is
preferable to a multinational force, and the introduction of a UN
force to replace the MFO remains a diplomatic goal of Egyptian
policy.[12]

The Director-General of the MFO believes that the UN remains
the appropriate peacekeeping mechanism for world issues, and that a
non-UN force is called for only in those instances where political
problems within the UN make it impossible for the latter to
undertake peacekeeping duties. The MFO has certain advantages
over a large multi-purpose institution, including direct funding, a
limited number of masters, and clearly established independence.
The MFO was tailor-made for a given set of circumstances. The

basis of its success, in his view, is that the Force was able to respond to a mandate given to it by two strong Governments, and one to which they were committed. In order to fulfill a task in a different area and situation, a new format would have to be worked out. The prerequisite for peacekeeping is always "two determined nations prepared to give full support to the effort."[13] Given the situation in Lebanon, for example, the circumstances are much more complicated, and therefore the chances for success more doubtful regardless of the nature of the force stationed there.

The purpose of the MFO is to supervise the security arrangements that Israel and Egypt took upon themselves under the 1979 Peace Treaty, as well as to ensure freedom of navigation in the Strait of Tiran, and as such to build good faith between the sides. The responsibilities of the MFO pertain only to the security arrangements provided by the Treaty, and not to the Treaty as a whole. To a certain extent the MFO was intended to serve as a guarantee to peace, in spite of the potentially volatile situations characteristic of the Middle East. It is clear that given the quantity and type of weapons it is permitted, the MFO is incapable of carrying out all the functions assigned to it, which in fact constitute part of the security arrangements. Doubts may be raised as to whether in case of serious Treaty violations the MFO's functions can be effectively carried out with the existing means and methods.

Within the MFO directorate, it is felt that for the function of observing and reporting, MFO weapons are adequate. If, on the other hand, five armored divisions were moved across the border, the MFO would require five divisions to stop them. The MFO can only make certain that the Peace Treaty is observed.

The MFO has no radar. The feeling is that it does not really require it. Electronic monitoring devices might have been used, in lieu of the MFO, but the parties preferred people to perform the monitoring function, and therefore the MFO was devised.

The MFO was not intended to serve as a fighting force or to repel regular armies.[14] The intention is for the MFO to uncover violations and to report them and demand that they be rectified.

Its strength lies not in its military capability, but in the support of the participating States and in its ability to serve as a deterrent.

The MFO serves as a safety valve that inhibits or renders more difficult a decision to violate the security arrangements. However, once a party reaches the decision to renounce the Treaty provisions, it would be beyond the power of the MFO to enforce adherence. Only a fighting force such as the UN Expeditionary Force in Korea consisting of combat units with a unified command under the US would have the mandate and means to compel the parties to adhere to the Treaty.

The Commander of the Force has stated that violations of the Peace Treaty do occur, but publicizing them might be used politically by one party or the other.[15] The MFO would like to describe and report, and to refrain from assigning grades for the performance of the parties or to characterize the relative degree of gravity of violations. The Force Commander has formally noted violations on several occasions, but announcements to this effect are made privately to the parties, and the figures are not tabulated. Violations, mostly by Israeli planes and by Egyptian patrols, have "all been very minor, administrative errors, technical in nature, and there have been immediate steps on both sides to attempt to rectify, where that was pertinent, any violations." The MFO attributes these violations partly to the fact that both Egypt and Israel use a lot of reserve military people and that they are both new to the requirements of the Treaty and the Protocol.[16]

At the beginning of February 1984 Israel asked the MFO to ensure that Egypt does not create a greater military infrastructure in Zone A than is allowed under the provisions of the peace package. Israel was apparently concerned over the fact that while the Egyptians have been careful not to station more than the specified one division in Zone A, they undertook an extensive building program, possibly laying a military infrastructure capable of containing a larger force. Israel was particularly sensitive to such changes, against the background of minimal diplomatic contact between the two countries (Egypt withdrew its ambassador from Israel) and rapprochement between Egypt and the Arab countries (Egypt rejoined the Islamic Conference Organization).[17]

The key to the establishment, functioning, continuation and success of the Force is the United States. The latter has committed its political prestige, as well as organizational skill, manpower and funds to the MFO. At the same time, the key role of the US deterred many States from participating in the MFO, lest the Force be perceived as a cover-up for the establishment of US bases in the Sinai for the US Rapid Deployment Forces (RDF). The US Congress in a resolution expressed reservations to ensure that the MFO not turn into an exclusively American force. A variety of doubts were voiced in Congress:

> If we are going to send ... American troops over there, I want to make sure that they can defend themselves totally ... can they work in conjunction with other nations and a commander who will not be an American? And can they work in harmony, especially in a situation that may occur at night in a very scattered type of situation, for example, with some sort of terrorist groups?[18]

Through participation in the MFO the US renewed its commitment to the peace process. The US presence in the Sinai constitutes an effective deterrent against serious violations of the Treaty, and as a moderating factor against a possible Israeli reaction to "light" violations by Egypt. Thus the importance of the arrangement calling for effective liaison and cooperation between the MFO and the parties.[19] The participation of a respectable number of countries in the MFO, including four European Community States, has contributed to its multinational status. It was initially feared that the difficulties posed by the Europeans before joining the Force were indicative of the fact that they would serve as a destabilizing factor in the face of subsequent crises, particularly concerning the Palestinian question and the issue of Egypt's inter-Arab relations.[20]

The specter of possible withdrawal of contingents initially concerned the Israeli Government. Some Israeli policy-makers noted that the European contingents could never be as reliable as regards Israel's vital interests as the contingents from the US, Colombia and Fiji, because of the European Governments' policies towards the Arabs. Israel envisaged a situation in which freedom of navigation in the Strait of Tiran was in jeopardy and simultaneously one or all of the Four would consider continued participation in the Force as conflicting with their own interests in the Arab world. Australian Prime Minister Malcolm Fraser stated that his country's contingent commander might conceivably have to consult his Government before obeying an order from the Sinai force commander. The Governments of Fiji and Colombia reserved the right to withdraw contingents on reasonable notice, allowing time for replacement countries to be found.[21] In this respect, too, there have not been problems to date.

The MFO has succeeded thus far perhaps because the setting in which it has functioned has been relatively peaceful. The potential problems envisaged have meanwhile not materialized: lack of cooperation by one of the parties to the Peace Treaty; insubordination of participating States (since a suitable replacement has been found for Australia, when it withdraws, the integrity of the MFO has not been affected); terrorist infiltration and sabotage in the peacekeeping area; budgetary problems and others.

Or perhaps, like the lighthouse at sea, the very presence of the MFO has deterred problems that otherwise might have arisen. Along with the verification function established in the Peace Treaty, there is the physical presence of the Force which the parties intended as a deterrent more effective than the most sophisticated electronic monitoring. In either case, the MFO constitutes a novel approach to international peacekeeping, a triumph of "creative diplomacy" devoid of many of the problems recently faced by UN-sponsored forces -- namely, Communist and Third-World pressures. All sides stand to gain from the success of the Force -- Egypt and Israel will maintain their hard-earned peace, the United States will have stood by its commitment to uphold that peace, and the other contributing States will have played a role in an enterprise of international significance.

The task of the MFO is limited to "peacekeeping." It bolsters and builds confidence in the stability of an already established arrangement. As such it might serve as a prototype for similar forces in other areas where peacekeeping is required. An example might be a multinational force in Chad with appropriate political backing. Where the situation is more volatile, however, as in Lebanon, it is clear that such a force alone cannot be effective at "peacemaking." The ultimate success of the Force will be at the point where the parties will decide that they can live side by side without any force at all.

NOTES

(1)   "The Multinational Force" (Hebrew), Ma'arachot (No. 283) 28 (July 1982).
(2) MFO Annual Report, 1983, p. 6.
(3) Ibid., p. 8.
(4) MFO Annual Report, 1983, p. 8.
The USSR has expressed its opposition to the MFO. Early in 1982, Constantin Chernenko criticized the Force and suggested that instead an international conference be called for, with the participation of Syria, Lebanon, Jordan, Egypt, the PLO, Israel, the USSR, the US, and States representing areas connected wih the Middle East, Western Europe, South Asia and North Africa. (Interview to L'Attitude, cited in Ma'ariv, Feb. 16, 1982, p. 6.) Izvestia wrote that the plan to constitute a multinational force was nothing more than part of a NATO scheme to guarantee US influence in the Middle East (Haaretz, Nov. 1, 1981). Tass, the Soviet news agency, accused the US of taking over through the MFO, and that Egyptian sovereignty was being limited (Nov. 1, 1980). The French Communist Party, a partner in the country's Socialist Government, opposed participation in the MFO. It did not see any good purpose in risking its good relations with the Arab world, and doubted that it was the right time for France to get involved in the Camp David process. (L'Humanité cited in Haaretz, Nov. 3, 1981, p. 2). On Soviet non-participation see also MFO House Hearings, pp. 56-57.
(5) Pelcovits, p. 69. Initially Egypt was unhappy about the MFO's open-ended term (ibid., p. 70).
(6) On the MNF see Pelcovits, Chs. 4, 5. Appendix B. James A. Phillips, "Standing Firm in Lebanon," Heritage Foundation Backgrounder (No. 302) (Oct. 28, 1983).

(7) Professor Ruth Lapidoth points out two differences between the Peace Treaty provisions and the MFO:

1. The Peace Treaty prohibits participation of the 5 permanent members of the Security Council in the force, whereas the MFO includes the US, UK and France;

2. The Peace Treaty provides for the cessation of US surveillance flights after Israel's withdrawal to the international border, while the exchange of letters provides for their continuation. For a legal analysis, see Lapidoth, pp. 374 ff.

(8) Ramesh Thakur, "The Olive Branch Brigades: Peacekeeping in the Middle East," 40 The World Today (No. 3) 93, at 97 (March 1984).

(9) Roger A. Brooks, "U.N. Peacekeeping: An Empty Mandate," Heritage Foundation Backgrounder (No. 262) (April 20, 1983).

(10) According to the Report, there was close and systematic cooperation between UNIFIL personnel and the PLO, and the former even passed intelligence information to the PLO on a regular basis. On one occasion the PLO was able to induce UNIFIL to supply it with sophisticated communication equipment. Fully armed PLO liaison officers were permitted to move with an armed escort through UNIFIL "controlled" territory. Explosives were allegedly carried into Israel by individual UNIFIL officers for use by PLO terrorists. UNIFIL officers were persuaded by the PLO to inform village leaders 24 hours in advance of any impending search for concealed weapons.

(11) See Lapidoth, pp. 387-88.

(12) October, Dec. 9, 1984 (Arabic).

(13) Hunt Press Conference, Jan. 17, 1983, p. 12.

(14) "The Multinational Force" (Hebrew), Ma'arachot (No. 283) 30 (July 1982).

(15) Jerusalem Post, April 22, 1983, p. 7.

(16) Hunt Press Conference, Jan. 17, 1983, p. 8. Terence Smith, New York Times, Nov. 25, 1983, p. A 10. See James, p. 17.

(17) Hirsh Goodman, Jerusalem Post, Feb. 3, 1984, p. 1.

(18) MFO House Hearings, p. 20.

(19) Ma'arachot, supra note 14, p. 30; MFO House Hearings, p. 63.

(20) Ibid.

(21) Jerusalem Post, April 27, 1981, p. 1.

Appendix A
A Treaty of Peace

These Appendixes present those documents most relevant to the establishment and mission of the Multinational Force and Observers. It should not be considered a definite collection of all the documentation relating to the Peace Treaty of March 26, 1979.

The appendixes are reproduced from: *Annual Report of the Director General, Multinational Force and Observers*, April 25, 1983, pp. 31-63; April 25, 1984, pp. 35-40.

Treaty of Peace between the Arab Republic of Egypt and the State of Israel

The Government of the Arab Republic of Egypt and the Government of the State of Israel:

PREAMBLE

Convinced of the urgent necessity of the establishment of a just, comprehensive and lasting peace in the Middle East in accordance with Security Council Resolutions 242 and 338:

Reaffirming their adherence to the "Framework for Peace in the Middle East Agreed at Camp David" dated September 17, 1978:

Noting that the aforementioned Framework as appropriate is intended to constitute a basis for peace not only between Egypt and Israel but also between Israel and each of its other Arab neighbors which is prepared to negotiate peace with it on this basis:

Desiring to bring to an end the state of war between them and to establish a peace in which every state in the area can live in security:

Convinced that the conclusion of a Treaty of Peace between Egypt and Israel is an important step in the search for comprehensive peace in the area and for the attainment of the settlement of the Arab-Israeli conflict in all its aspects:

Inviting the other Arab parties to this dispute to join the peace process with Israel guided by and based on the principles of the aforementioned Framework:

Desiring as well to develop friendly relations and cooperation between themselves in accordance with the United Nations Charter and the principles of international law governing international relations in times of peace:

Agree to the following provisions in the free exercise of their sovereignty, in order to implement the "Framework for the Conclusion of a Peace Treaty between Egypt and Israel".

ARTICLE I

1. The state of war between the Parties will be terminated and peace will be established between them upon the exchange of instruments of ratification of this Treaty.

2. Israel will withdraw all its armed forces and civilians from the Sinai behind the international boundary between Egypt and mandated Palestine, as provided in the annexed protocol (Annex I), and Egypt will resume the exercise of its full sovereignty over the Sinai.

3. Upon completion of the interim withdrawal provided for in Annex I, the Parties will establish normal and friendly relations, in accordance with Article III (3).

ARTICLE II

The permanent boundary between Egypt and Israel is the recognized international boundary between Egypt and the former mandated territory of Palestine, as shown on the map at Annex II, without prejudice to the issue of the status of the Gaza Strip. The Parties recognize this boundary as inviolable. Each will respect the territorial integrity of the other, including their territorial waters and airspace.

ARTICLE III

1. The Parties will apply between them the provisions of the Charter of the United Nations and the principles of the international law governing relations among states in times of peace. In particular:

a. The recognize and will respect each other's sovereignty, territorial integrity and political independence;

b. They recognize and will respect each other's right to live in peace within their secure and recognized boundaries;

c. They will refrain from the threat or use of force, directly or indirectly, against each other and will settle all disputes between them by peaceful means.

2. Each Party undertakes to ensure that acts or threats of belligerency, or violence do not originate from and are not committed from within its territory, or by any forces subject to its control or by any other forces stationed on its territory, against the population, citizens or property of the other Party. Each Party also undertakes to refrain from organizing, instigating, inciting, assisting or participating in acts or threats of belligerency, hostility, subversion or violence against the other Party,

anywhere, and undertakes to ensure that perpetrators of such acts are brought to justice.

3. The Parties agree that the normal relationship established between them will include full recognition, diplomatic, economic and cultural relations, termination of economic boycotts and discriminatory barriers to the free movement of people and goods, and will guarantee the mutual enjoyment by citizens of the due process of law. The process by which they undertake to achieve such a relationship parallel of this Treaty is set out in the annexed protocol (Annex III).

ARTICLE IV

1. In order to provide maximum security for both Parties on the basis of reciprocity, agreed security arrangements will be established including limited force zones in Egyptian and Israeli territory, and United Nations forces and observers, described in detail as to nature and timing in Annex I, and other security arrangements the Parties may agree upon.

2. The Parties agree to the stationing of United Nations personnel in areas described in Annex I. The Parties agree not to request withdrawal of the United Nations personnel and that these personnel will not be removed unless such removal is approved by the Security Council of the United Nations, with the affirmative vote of the five Permanent Members, unless the Parties otherwise agree.

3. A Joint Commission will be established to facilitate the implementation of the Treaty, as provided for in Annex I.

4. The security arrangements provided for in paragraph 1 and 2 of this Article may at the request of either party be reviewed and amended by mutual agreement of the Parties.

ARTICLE V

1. Ships of Israel, and cargoes destined for or coming from Israel, shall enjoy the right of free passage through the Suez Canal and its approaches through the Gulf of Suez and the Mediterranean Sea on the basis of the Constantinople Convention of 1888, applying to all nations. Israeli nationals, vessels and cargoes, as well as persons, vessels and cargoes destined for or coming from Israel, shall be accorded non-discriminatory treatment in all matters connected with usage of the canal.

2. The Parties consider the Strait of Tiran and the Gulf of Aqaba to be international waterways open to all nations for unimpeded and non-suspendable freedom of navigation and overflight. The Parties will respect each other's right to navigation and overflight for access to either country through the Strait of Tiran and the Gulf of Aqaba.

ARTICLE VI

1. This Treaty does not affect and shall not be interpreted as affecting in any way the rights and obligations of the Parties under the Charter of the United Nations.

2. The Parties undertake to fulfill in good faith their obligations under this Treaty, without regard to action or inaction of any other party and independently of any instrument external to this Treaty.

3. They further undertake to take all the necessary measures for the application in their relations of the provisions of the multilateral conventions to which they are parties, including the submission of appropriate notification to the Secretary General of the United Nations and other depositaries of such conventions.

4. The Parties undertake not to enter into any obligation in conflict with this Treaty.

5. Subject to Article 103 of the United Nations Charter, in the event of a conflict between the obligations of the Parties under the present Treaty and any of their other obligations, the obligations under this Treaty will be binding and implemented.

ARTICLE VII

1. Disputes arising out of the application or interpretation of this Treaty shall be resolved by negotiations.

2. Any such disputes which cannot be settled by negotiations shall be resolved by conciliation or submitted to arbitration.

ARTICLE VIII

The Parties agree to establish a claims commission for the mutual settlement of all financial claims.

ARTICLE IX

1. This Treaty shall enter into force upon exchange of instruments of ratification.

2. This Treaty supersedes the Agreement between Egypt and Israel of September, 1975.

3. All protocols, annexes, and maps attached to this Treaty shall be regarded as an integral part hereof.

4. The Treaty shall be communicated to the Secretary General of the United Nations for registration in accordance with the provisions of Article 102 of the Charter of the United Nations.

DONE at Washington, D.C. this 26th day of March, 1979, in triplicate in the English, Arabic, and Hebrew languages, each text being equally authentic. In case of any divergence of interpretation, the English text shall prevail.

For the Government of the
Arab Republic of Egypt:

s/Mohamed Anwar El-Sadat

For the Government
of Israel:

s/Menachem Begin

Witnessed by:

s/Jimmy Carter, President
of the United States of America

ANNEX I

PROTOCOL CONCERNING ISRAELI
WITHDRAWAL AND SECURITY
ARRANGEMENTS

Article I
Concept of Withdrawal

1. Israel will complete withdrawal of all its armed forces and civilians from the Sinai not later than three years from the date of exchange of instruments of ratification of this Treaty.

2. To ensure the mutual security of the Parties, the implementation of phased withdrawal will be accompanied by the military measures and establishment of zones set out in this Annex and in Map 1, hereinafter referred to as "the Zones."

3. The withdrawal from the Sinai will be accomplished in two phases:

a. The interim withdrawal behind the line from east of El Arish to Ras Muhammed as delineated on Map 2 within nine months from the date of exchange of instruments of ratification of this Treaty.
b. The final withdrawal from the Sinai behind the international boundary not later than three years from the date of exchange of instruments of ratification of this Treaty.

4. A Joint Commission will be formed immediately after the exchange of instruments of ratification of this Treaty in order to supervise and coordinate movements and schedules during the withdrawal, and to adjust plans and timetables as necessary within the limits established by paragraph 3, above. Details relating to the Joint Commission are set out in Article IV of the attached Appendix. The Joint Commission will be dissolved upon completion of final Israeli withdrawal from the Sinai.

Article II
Determination of Final Lines and Zones

1. In order to provide maximum security for both Parties after the final withdrawal, the lines and the Zones delineated on Map 1 are to be established and organized as follows:

a. Zone A
(1) Zone A is bounded on the east by line A (red line) and on the west by the Suez Canal and the east coast of the Gulf of Suez, as shown on Map 1.

(2) An Egyptian armed force of one mechanized infantry division and its military installations, and field fortifications, will be in this Zone.
(3) The main elements of that Division will consist of:
(a) Three mechanized infantry brigades.
(b) One armored brigade.
(c) Seven field artillery battalions including up to 126 artillery pieces.
(d) Seven anti-aircraft artillery battalions including individual surface-to-air missiles and up to 126 anti-aircraft guns of 37 mm and above.
(e) Up to 230 tanks.
(f) Up to 480 armored personnel vehicles of all types.
(g) Up to a total of twenty-two thousand personnel.

b. Zone B
(1) Zone B is bounded by line B (green line) on the east and by line A (red line) on the west, as shown on Map 1.
(2) Egyptian border units of four battalions equipped with light weapons and wheeled vehicles will provide security and supplement the civil police in maintaining order in Zone B. The main elements of the four Border Battalions will consist of up to a total of four thousand personnel.
(3) Land based, short range, low power, coastal warning points of the border patrol units may be established on the coast of this Zone.
(4) There will be in Zone B field fortifications and military installations for the four border battalions.

c. Zone C
(1) Zone C is bounded by line B (green line) on the west and the International Boundary and the Gulf of Aqaba on the east, as shown on Map 1.
(2) Only United Nations forces and Egyptian civil police will be stationed in Zone C.
(3) The Egyptian civil police armed with light weapons will perform normal police functions within this Zone.
(4) The United Nations Force will be deployed within Zone C and perform its functions as defined in Article VI of the Annex.
(5) The United Nations Force will be stationed mainly in camps located within the following

stationing areas shown on Map 1, and will establish its precise locations after consultations with Egypt:

(a) In the part of the area in the Sinai lying within about 20 km. of the Mediterranean Sea and adjacent to the International Boundary.

(b) In the Sharm el Sheikh area.

d. Zone D

(1) Zone D is bounded by line D (blue line) on the east and the International Boundary on the west, as shown on Map 1.

(2) In this Zone there will be an Israeli limited force of four infantry battalions, their military installations, and field fortifications, and United Nations observers.

(3) The Israeli forces in Zone D will not include tanks, artillery and anti-aircraft missiles except individual surface-to-air missiles.

(4) The main elements of the four Israeli infantry battalions will consist of up to 180 armored personnel vehicles of all types and up to a total of four thousand personnel.

2. Access accross the international boundary shall only be permitted through entry check points designated by each Party and under its control. Such access shall be in accordance with laws and regulations of each country.

3. Only those field fortifications, military installations, forces and weapons specifically permitted by this Annex shall be in the Zones.

Article III
Aerial Military Regime

1. Flights of combat aircraft and reconnaisance flights of Egypt and Israel shall take place only over Zones A and D, respectively.

2. Only unarmed, non-combat aircraft of Egypt and Israel will be stationed in Zones A and D, respectively.

3. Only Egyptian unarmed transport aircraft will take off and land in Zone B and up to eight such aircraft may be maintained in Zone B. The Egyptian border units may be equipped with unarmed helicopters to perform their functions in Zone B.

4. The Egyptian civil police may be equipped with unarmed police helicopters to perform normal police functions in Zone C.

5. Only civilian airfields may be built in the Zones.

6. Without prejudice to the provisions of this Treaty, only those military aerial activities specifically permitted by this Annex shall be allowed in the Zones and the airspace above their territorial waters.

Article IV
Naval Regime

1. Egypt and Israel may base and operate naval vessels along the coasts of Zones A and D, respectively.

2. Egyptians coast guard boats, lightly armed, may be stationed and operate in the territorial waters of Zone B to assist the border units in performing their functions in this Zone.

3. Egyptian civil police equipped with light boats, lightly armed, shall perform normal police functions within the territorial waters of Zone C.

4. Nothing in this Annex shall be considered as derogating from the right of innocent passage of the naval vessels of either party.

5. Only civilian maritime ports and installations may be built in the Zones.

6. Withouth prejudice to the provisions of this Treaty, only those naval activities specifically permitted by this Annex shall be allowed in the Zones and in their territorial waters.

Article V
Early Warning Systems

Egypt and Israel may establish and operate early warning systems only in Zones A and D respectively.

Article VI
United Nations Operations

1. The Parties will request the United Nations to provide forces and observers to supervise the implementation of this Annex and employ their best efforts to prevent any violation of its terms.

2. With respect to these United Nations forces and observers, as appropriate, the Parties agree to request the following arrangements:

a. Operation of check points, reconnaissance patrols, and observation posts along the international boundary and line B, and within Zone C.

b. Periodic verification of the implementation of the provisions of this Annex will be carried out not less than twice a month unless otherwise agreed by the Parties.

c. Additional verifications within 48 hours after the receipt of a request from either Party.

d. Ensuring the freedom of navigation through the Strait of Tiran in accordance with Article V of the Treaty of Peace.

3. The arrangements described in this article for each zone will be implemented in Zones A, B, and C by the United Nations Force and in Zone D by the United Nations Observers.

4. United Nations verification teams shall be accompanied by liaison officers of the respective Party.

5. The United Nations Force and Observers will report their findings to both Parties.

6. The United Nations Force and Observers operating in the Zones will enjoy freedom of movement and other facilities necessary for the performance of their tasks.

7. The United Nations Force and Observers are not empowered to authorize the crossing of the international boundary.

8. The Parties shall agree on the nations from which the United Nations Force and Observers will be drawn. They will be drawn from nations other than those which are permanent members of the United Nations Security Council.

9. The Parties agree that the United Nations should make those command arrangements that will best assure the effective implementation of its responsibilities.

Article VII
Liaison System

1. Upon dissolution of the Joint Commission, a liaison system between the Parties will be established. This liaison system is intended to provide an effective method to assess progress in the implementation of obligations under the present Annex and to resolve any problem that may arise in the course of implementation, and refer other unresolved matters to the higher military authorities of the two countries respectively for consideration. It is also intended to prevent situations resulting from errors or misinterpretation on the part of either Party.

2. An Egyptian liaison office will be established in the city of El Arish and an Israeli liaison office will be established in the city of Beer-Sheba. Each office will be headed by an officer of the respective country, and assisted by a number of officers.

3. A direct telephone link between the two offices will be set up and also direct telephone lines with the United Nations command will be maintained by both offices.

Article VIII
Respect for War Memorials

Each Party undertakes to preserve in good condition the War Memorials erected in the memory of soldiers of the other Party, namely those erected by Israel in the Sinai and those to be erected by Egypt in Israel and shall permit access to such monuments.

Article IX
Interim Arrangements

The withdrawal of Israeli armed forces and civilians behind the interim withdrawal line, and the conduct of the forces of the Parties and the United Nations prior to the final withdrawal, will be governed by the attached Appendix and Maps 2 and 3.

APPENDIX TO ANNEX I

ORGANIZATION OF MOVEMENTS IN THE SINAI

Article I
Principles of Withdrawal

1. The withdrawal of Israeli armed forces and civilians from the Sinai will be accomplished in two phases as described in Article I of Annex I. The description and timing of the withdrawal are included in this Appendix. The Joint Commission will develop and present to the Chief Coordinator of the United Nations forces in the Middle East the details of these phases not later than one month before the initiation of each phase of withdrawal.

2. Both Parties agree on the following principles for the sequence of military movements.

a. Notwithstanding the provisions of Article IX, paragraph 2, of this Treaty, until Israeli armed forces complete withdrawal from the current J and M Lines established by the Egyptian-Israeli Agreement of September 1975, hereinafter referred to as the 1975 Agreement, up to the interim withdrawal line, all military arrangements existing under that Agreement will remain in effect, except those military arrangements otherwise provided for in this Appendix.

b. As Israeli armed forces withdraw, United Nations forces will immediately enter the evacuated areas to establish interim and temporary buffer zones as shown on Maps 2 and 3, respectively, for the purpose of maintaining a separation of forces. United Nations forces' deployment will precede the movement of any other personnel into these areas.

c. Within a period of seven days after Israeli armed forces have evacuated any area located in Zone A, units of Egyptian armed forces shall deploy in accordance with the provisions of Article II of this Appendix.

d. Within a period of seven days after Israeli armed forces have evacuated any area located in Zones A or B, Egyptian border units shall deploy in accordance with the provisions of Article II of this Appendix, and will function in accordance with the provisions of Article II of Annex I.

e. Egyptian civil police will enter evacuated areas immediately after the United Nations forces to perform normal police functions.

f. Egyptian naval units shall deploy in the Gulf of Suez in accordance with the provisions of Article II of this Appendix.

g. Except those movements mentioned above, deployments of Egyptian armed forces and the activities covered in Annex I will be effected in the evacuated areas when Israeli armed forces have completed their withdrawal behind the interim withdrawal line.

Article II
Subphases of the Withdrawal to the Interim Withdrawal Line

1. The withdrawal to the interim withdrawal line will be accomplished in subphases as described in this Article and as shown on Map 3. Each subphase will be completed within the indicated number of months from the date of the exchange of instruments of ratification of this Treaty.

a. First subphase: within two months, Israeli armed forces will withdraw from the area of El Arish, including the town of El Arish and its airfield, shown as Area I on Map 3.

b. Second subphase: within three months, Israeli armed forces will withdraw from the area between line M of the 1975 Agrement and line A, shown as Area II on Map 3.

c. Third subphase: within five months, Israeli armed forces will withdraw from the areas east and south of Area II, shown as Area III on Map 3.

d. Fourth subphase: within seven months, Israeli armed forces will withdraw from the area of El Tor - Ras El Kenisa, shown as Area IV on Map 3.

e. Fifth subphase: Within nine months, Israeli armed forces will withdraw from the remaining areas west of the interim withdrawal line, including the areas of Santa Katrina and the areas east of the Giddi and Mitla passes, shown as Area V on Map 3, thereby completing Israeli withdrawal behind the interim withdrawal line.

2. Egyptian forces will deploy in the areas evacuated by Israeli armed forces as follows:

a. Up to one-third of the Egyptian armed forces in the Sinai in accordance with the 1975 Agreement will deploy in the portions of Zone A lying within Area I, until the completion of interim withdrawal. Thereafter, Egyptian armed forces as described in Article II of Annex I will be deployed in Zone A up to the limits of the interim buffer zone.

b. The Egyptian naval activity in accordance with Article IV of Annex I will commence along the coasts of Areas II, III, and IV, upon completion of the second, third, and fourth subphases, respectively.

c. Of the Egyptian border units described in Article II of Annex I, upon completion of the first subphase one battalion will be deployed in Area I. A second battalion will be deployed in Area II upon completion of the second subphase. A third battalion will be deployed in Area III upon completion of the third subphase. The second and third battalions mentioned above may also be deployed in any of the subsequently evacuated areas of the southern Sinai.

3. United Nations forces in Buffer Zone I of the 1975 Agreement will redeploy to enable the deployment of Egyptian forces described above upon the completion of the first subphase, but will otherwise continue to function in accordance with the provisions of that Agreement in the remainder of that zone until the completion of interim withdrawal, as indicated in Article I of this Appendix.

4. Israeli convoys may use the roads south and east of the main road junction east of El Arish to evacuate Israeli forces and equipment up to the completion of interim withdrawal. These convoys will proceed in daylight upon four hour notice to the Egyptian liaison group and United Nations forces, will be escorted by United Nations forces, and will be in accordance with schedules coordinated by the Joint Commission. An Egyptian liaison officer will accompany convoys to assure uninterrupted movement. The Joint Commission may approve other arrangements for convoys.

Article III
United Nations Forces

1. The Parties shall request that United Nations forces be deployed as necessary to perform the functions described in this Appendix up to the time of completion of final Israeli withdrawal.

For that purpose, the Parties agree to the redeployment of the United Nations Emergency Force.

2. United Nations forces will supervise the implementation of this Appendix and will employ their best efforts to prevent any violation of its terms.

3. When United Nations forces deploy in accordance with the provisions of Articles I and II of this Appendix, they will perform the functions of verification in limited force zones in accordance with Article VI of Annex I, and will establish check points, reconnaissance patrols, and observation posts in the temporary buffer zones described in Article II above. Other functions of the United Nations forces which concern the interim buffer zone are described in Article V of this Appendix.

Article IV
Joint Commission and Liaison

1. The Joint Commission referred to in Article IV of this Treaty will function from the date of exchange of instruments of ratification of this Treaty up to the date of completion of final Israel withdrawal from the Sinai.

2. The Joint Commission will be composed of representatives of each Party headed by senior officers. This Commission shall invite a representative of the United Nations when discussing subjects concerning the United Nations, or when either Party requests United Nations presence. Decisions of the Joint Commission will be reached by agreement of Egypt and Israel.

3. The Joint Commission will supervise the implementation of the arrangements described in Annex I and this Appendix. To this end, and by agreement of both Parties, it will:

a. Coordinate military movements described in this Appendix and supervise their implementation;
b. Address and seek to resolve any problem arising out of the implementation of Annex I and this Appendix, and discuss any violations reported by the United Nations Force and Observers and refer to the Governments of Egypt and Israel any unresolved problems;
c. Assist the United Nations Force and Observers in the execution of their mandates, and deal with the timetables of the periodic verifications when referred to it by the Parties as provided for in Annex I and in this Appendix;
d. Organize the demarcation of the international boundary and all lines and zones described in Annex I and this Appendix;
e. Supervise the handing over of the main installations in the Sinai from Israel to Egypt;
f. Agree on necessary arrangements for finding and returning missing bodies of Egyptian and Israeli soldiers;

g. Organize the setting up and operation of entry check points along the El Arish - Ras Muhammed line in accordance with the provisions of Article 4 of Annex III;
h. Conduct its operations through the use of joint liaison teams consisting of one Israeli representative and one Egyptian representative, provided from a standing Liaison Group, which will conduct activities as directed by the Joint Commission;
i. Provide liaison and coordination to the United Nations command implementing provisions of the Treaty, and, through the joint liaison teams, maintain local coordination and cooperation with the United Nations Force stationed in specific areas for any assistance as needed;
j. Discuss any other matters which the Parties by agreement may place before it.

4. Meetings of the Joint Commission shall be held at least once a month. In the event that either Party or the Command of the United Nations Force requests a special meeting, it will be convened within 24 hours,.

5. The Joint Commission will meet in the buffer zone until the completion of the interim withdrawal and in El Arish and Beer-Sheba alternately afterwards. The first meeting will be held not later than two weeks after the entry into force of this Treaty.

Article V
Definition of the Interim Buffer Zone and Its Activities

1. An interim buffer zone, by which the United Nations Force will effect a separation of Egyptian and Israeli elements, will be established west of and adjacent to the interim withdrawal line as shown on Map 2 after implementation of Israeli withdrawal and deployment behind the interim withdrawal line. Egyptian civil police equipped with light weapons will perform normal police functions within this zone.

2. The United Nations Force will operate check points, reconnaissance patrols, and observation posts within the interim buffer zone in order to ensure compliance with the terms of this Article.

3. In accordance with arrangements agreed upon by both Parties and to be coordinated by the Joint Commission, Israeli personnel will operate military technical installations at four specific locations shown on Map 2 and designated as T1 (map central coordinate 57163940), T2 (map central coordinate 59351541), T3 (map central coordinate 59331527), and T4 (map central coordinate 61130979) under the following principles:

a. The technical installations shall be manned by technical and administrative personnel equipped with small arms required for their protection (revolvers, rifles, sub-machine guns, light machine guns, hand grenades, and ammunition), as follows:

> T1 - up to 150 personnel
> T2 and T3 - up to 350 personnel
> T4 - up to 200 personnel.

b. Israeli personnel will not carry weapons outside the sites, except officers who may carry personal weapons.
c. Only a third party agreed to by Egypt and Israel will enter and conduct inspections within the perimeters of technical installations in the buffer zone. The third party will conduct inspections in a random manner at least once a month. The inspections will verify the nature of the operation of the installations and the weapons and personnel therein. The third party will immediately report to the Parties any divergence from an installation's visual and electronic surveillance or communications role.
d. Supply of the installations, visits for technical and administrative purposes, and replacement of personnel and equipment situated in the sites, may occur uninterruptedly from the United Nations check points to the perimeter of the technical installations, after checking and being escorted by only the United Nations forces.
e. Israel will be permitted to introduce into its technical installations items required for the proper functioning of the installations and personnel.
f. As determined by the Joint Commission, Israel will be permitted to:

(1) Maintain in its installations fire-fighting and general maintenance equipment as well as wheeled administrative vehicles and mobile engineering equipment necessary for the maintenance of the sites. All vehicles shall be unarmed.
(2) Within the sites and in the buffer zone, maintain roads, water lines, and communications cables which serve the sites. At each of the three installation locations (T1, T2 and T3, and T4), this maintenance may be performed with up to two unarmed wheeled vehicles and by up to twelve unarmed personnel with only necessary equipment, including heavy engineering equipment if needed. This maintenance may by performed three times a week, except for special problems, and only after giving the United Nations four hours notice.
The teams will be escorted by the United Nations.

g. Movement to and from the technical installations will take place only during daylight hours. Access to, and exit from, the technical installations shall be as follows:
(1) T1: through a United Nations check point, and via the road between Abu Aweigila and the intersection of the Abu Aweigila road and the Gebel Libni road (at km. 161), as shown on Map 2.
(2) T2 and T3: through a United Nations checkpoint and via the road constructed across the buffer zone to Gebel Katrina, as shown on Map 2.
(3) T2, T3, and T4: via helicopters flying within a corridor at the times, and according to a flight profile, agreed to by the Joint Commission. The helicopters will be checked by the United Nations Force at landing sites outside the perimeter of the installations.

h. Israel will inform the United Nations Force at least one hour in advance of each intended movement to and from the installations.
i. Israel shall be entitled to evacuate sick and wounded and summon medical experts and medical teams at any time after giving immediate notice to the United Nations Force.

4. The details of the above principles and all other matters in this Article requiring coordination by the Parties will be handled by the Joint Commission.

5. These technical installations will be withdrawn when Israeli forces withdraw from the interim withdrawal line, or at a time agreed by the Parties.

Article VI
Disposition of Installations and Military Barriers

Disposition of installations and military barriers will be determined by the Parties in accordance with the following guidelines:

1. Up to three weeks before Israeli withdrawal from any area, the Joint Commission will arrange for Israeli and Egyptian liaison and technical teams to conduct a joint inspection of all appropriate installations to agree upon condition of structures and articles which will be transferred to Egyptian control and to arrange for such transfer. Israel will declare, at that time, its plans for disposition of installations and articles within the installations.

2. Israel undertakes to transfer to Egypt all agreed infrastructure, utilities, and installations intact, inter alia, airfields, roads, pumping stations, and ports. Israel will present to Egypt the information necessary for the maintenance and operation of these facilities. Egyptian

technical teams will be permitted to observe and familiarize themselves with the operation of these facilities for a period of up to two weeks prior to transfer.

3. When Israel relinquishes Israeli military water points near El Arish and El Tor, Egyptian technical teams will assume control of those installations and ancillary equipment in accordance with an orderly transfer process arranged beforehand by the Joint Commission. Egypt undertakes to continue to make available at all water supply points the normal quantity of currently available water up to the time Israel withdraws behind the international boundary, unless otherwise agreed in the Joint Commission.

4. Israel will make its best effort to remove or destroy all military barriers, including obstacles and minefields, in the areas and adjacent waters from which it withdraws, according to the following concept:

a. Military barriers will be cleared first from areas near populations, roads, and major installations and utilities.
b. For those obstacles and minefields which cannot be removed or destroyed prior to Israeli withdrawal, Israel will provide detailed maps to Egypt and the United Nations through the Joint Commission not later than 15 days before entry of United Nations forces into the affected areas.
c. Egyptian military engineers will enter those areas after United Nations forces enter to conduct barrier clearance operations in accordance with Egyptian plans to be submitted prior to implementation.

Article VII
Surveillance Activities

1. Aerial surveillance activities during the withdrawal will be carried out as follows:

a. Both Parties request the United States to continue airborne surveillance flights in accordance with previous agreements until the completion of final Israeli withdrawal.
b. Flight profiles will cover the Limited Forces Zones to monitor the limitations on forces and armaments, and to determine that Israeli armed forces have withdrawn from the areas described in Article II of Annex I, Article II of this Appendix, and Maps 2 and 3, and that these forces thereafter remain behind their lines. Special inspection flights may be flown at the request of either Party or of the United Nations.
c. Only the main elements in the military organizations of each Party, as described in Annex I and in this Appendix, will be reported.

2. Both Parties request the United States operated Sinai Field Mission to continue its operations in accordance with previous agreements until completion of the Israeli withdrawal from the area east of the Giddi and Mitla Passes. Thereafter, the Mission will be terminated.

Article VIII
Exercise of Egyptian Sovereignty

Egypt will resume of its full sovereignty over evacuated parts of the Sinai upon Israeli withdrawal as provided for in Article I of this Treaty.

ANNEX III

PROTOCOL CONCERNING RELATIONS OF THE PARTIES

Article 1
Diplomatic and Consular Relations

The Farties agree to establish diplomatic and consular relations and to exchange ambassadors upon completion of the interim withdrawal.

Article 2
Economic and Trade Relations

1. The Parties agree to remove all discriminatory barriers to normal economic relations and to terminate economic boycotts of each other upon completion of the interim withdrawal.

2. As soon as possible, and not later than six months after the completion of the interim withdrawal, the Parties will enter negotiations with a view to concluding an agreement on trade and commerce for the purpose of promoting beneficial economic relations.

Article 3
Cultural Relations

1. The Parties agree to establish normal cultural relations following completion of the interim withdrawal.

2. They agree on the desirability of cultural exchanges in all fields, and shall, as soon as possible and not later than six months after completion of the interim withdrawal, enter into negotiations with a view to concluding a cultural agreement for this purpose.

Article 4
Freedom of Movement

1. Upon completion of the interim withdrawal, each Party will permit the free movement of the nationals and vehicles of the other into and within its territory according to the general rules applicable to nationals and vehicles of others states. Neither Party will impose discriminatory restrictions on the free movement of persons and vehicles from its territory to the territory of the other.

2. Mutual unimpeded access to places of religious and historical significance will be provided on a nondiscriminatory basis.

Article 5
Cooperation for Development and Good Neighborly Relations

1. The Parties recognize a mutuality of interest in good neighborly relations and agree to consider means to promote such relations.

2. The Parties will cooperate in promoting peace, stability and development in their region. Each agrees to consider proposals the other may wish to make to this end.

3. The Parties shall seek to foster mutual understanding and tolerance and will, accordingly, abstain from hostile propaganda against each other.

Article 6
Transportation and Telecommunications

1. The Parties recognize as applicable to each other the rights, privileges and obligations provided for by the aviation agreements to which they are both party, particularly by the Convention on International Civil Aviation, 1944 ("The Chicago Convention") and the International Air Services Transit Agreement, 1944.

2. Upon completion of the interim withdrawal any declaration of national emergency by a party under Article 89 of the Chicago Convention will not be applied to the other party on a discriminatory basis.

3. Egypt agrees that the use of airfields left by Israel near El Arish, Rafah, Ras El Nagb and Sharm El Sheikh shall be for civilian purposes only, including possible commercial use by all nations.

4. As soon as possible and not later than six months after the completion of the interim withdrawal, the Parties shall enter into negotiations for the purpose of concluding a civil aviation agreement.

5. The Parties will reopen and maintain roads and railways between their countries and will consider further road and rail links. The Parties further agree that a highway will be constructed and maintained between Egypt, Israel and Jordan near Eilat with guaranteed free and peaceful passage of persons, vehicles and goods between Egypt and Jordan, without

prejudice to their sovereignty over that part of the highway which falls within their respective territory.

6. Upon completion of the interim withdrawal, normal postal, telephone, telex, data facsimile, wireless and cable communications and television relay service by cable, radio and satellite shall be established between to two Parties in accordance with relevant international convention and regulations.

7. Upon completion of the interim withdrawal, each Party shall grant normal access to its ports for vessels and cargoes of the other, as well as vessels and cargoes destined for or coming from the other. Such access shall be granted on the same conditions generally applicable to vessels and cargoes of other nations. Article V of the Treaty of Peace will be implemented upon the exchange of instruments of ratifications of the aforementioned Treaty.

Article 7
Enjoyment of Human Rights

The Parties affirm their commitment to respect and observe human rights and fundamental freedoms for all and they will promote these rights and freedoms in accordance with the United Nations Charter.

Article 8
Territorial Seas

Without prejudice to the provisions of Article V of the Treaty of Peace each Party recognizes the right of the vessels of the other Party to innocent passage through its territorial sea in accordance with the rules of international law.

AGREED MINUTES TO ARTICLES I, IV, V AND VI AND ANNEXES I AND III OF TREATY OF PEACE

Article I

Egypt's resumption of the exercise of full sovereignty over the Sinai provided for in paragraph 2 of Article I shall occur with regard to each area upon Israel's withdrawal from that area.

Article IV

It is agreed between the Parties that the review provided for in Article IV (4) will be undertaken when requested by either Party, commencing within three months of such a request, but that any amendment can be made only with the mutual agreement of both Parties.

Article V

The second sentence of paragraph 2 of Article V shall not be construed as limiting the first sentence of that paragraph. The foregoing is not to be construed as contravening the second sentence of paragraph 2 of Article V, which reads as follows:

"The Parties will respect each other's right to navigation and overflight for access to either country through the Strait of Tiran and the Gulf of Aqaba."

Article VI (2)

The provisions of Article VI shall not be construed in contradiction to the provisions of the Framework for Peace in the Middle East agreed at Camp David. The foregoing is not to be construed as contravening the provisions of Article VI (2) of the Treaty, which reads as follows:

"The Parties undertake to fulfill in good faith their obligations under this Treaty, without regard to action or inaction of any other Party and independently of any instrument external to this Treaty."

Article VI (5)

It is agreed by the Parties that there is no assertion that this Treaty prevails over other treaties or agreements or that other treaties or agreements prevail over this Treaty. The foregoing is not to be construed as contravening the provisions of Article VI (5) of the Treaty, which reads as follows:

"Subject to Article 103 of the United Nations Charter, in the event of a conflict between the obligations of the Parties under the present Treaty and any of their other obligations, the obligations under this Treaty will be binding and implemented".

Annex I

Article VI, Paragraph 8, of Annex I provides as follows:

"The Parties shall agree on the nations from which the United National Force and Observers will be drawn. They will be drawn from nations other than those which are permanent members of the United Nations Security Council."

The Parties have agreed as follows:

"With respect to the provisions of paragraph 8, Article VI, of Annex I, if no agreement is reached between the Parties, they will accept or support a U.S. proposal concerning the composition of the United Nations Force and Observers."

Annex III

The Treaty of Peace and Annex III thereto provide for establishing normal economic relations between the Parties. In accordance therewith, it is agreed that such relations will include normal commercial sales of oil by Egypt to Israel, and that Israel shall be fully entitled to make bids for Egyptian-origin oil not needed for Egyptian domestic oil consumption, and Egypt and its oil concessionaires will entertain bids made by Israel, on the same basis and terms as apply to other bidders for such oil.

For the Goverment of Israel:
s/Menachem Begin

For the Government of the Arab Republic of Egypt:
s/Mohamed Anwar El-Sadat

Witnessed by:
s/Jimmy Carter, President of the United States of America

Appendix B
Maps of the Sinai

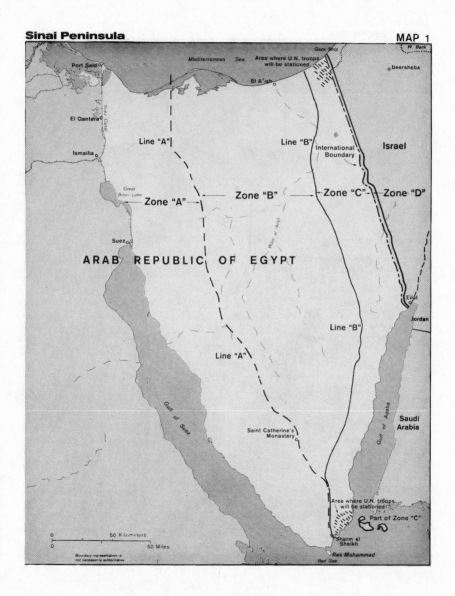

Sinai Peninsula

MAP 1

Mediterranean Sea

Port Said

El A'ish

El Qantara

Suez Canal

Ismailia

Line "A"

Line "B"

International Boundary

Israel

Beersheba

Gaza Strip

W. Bank

Area where U.N. troops will be stationed

Great Bitter Lake

Zone "A"

Zone "B"

Zone "C"

Zone "D"

Wadi el Arish

Suez

ARAB REPUBLIC OF EGYPT

Gulf of Suez

Line "A"

Line "B"

Eilat

Jordan

Gulf of Aqaba

Saudi Arabia

Saint Catherine's Monastery

0   50 Kilometers

0   50 Miles

Boundary representation is not necessarily authoritative

Area where U.N. troops will be stationed

Part of Zone "C"

Sharm el Sheikh

Ras Mohammad

Red Sea

141

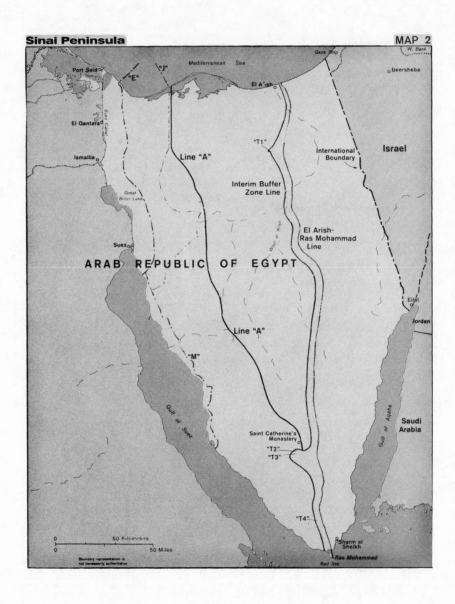

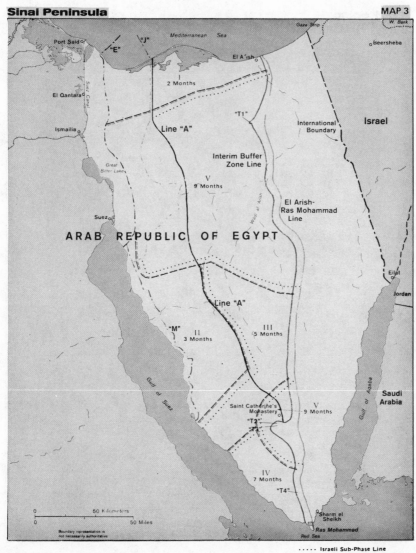

Sinai Peninsula MAP 3

144

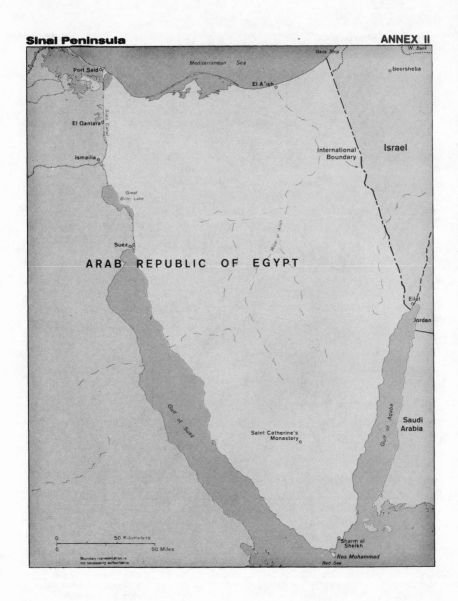

Appendix C
Protocol

Protocol

In view of the fact that the Egyptian-Israeli Treaty of Peace dated March 26, 1979 (hereinafter, "the Treaty"), provides for the fulfillment of certain functions by the United Nations Forces and Observers and that the President of the Security Council indicated on May 18, 1981, that the Security Council was unable to reach the necessary agreement on the proposal to establish the UN Forces and Observers, Egypt and Israel, acting in full respect of the purposes and principles of the United Nations Charter, have reached the following agreement:

1. A Multinational Force and Observers (hereinafter, "MFO") is hereby established as an alternative to the United Nations Forces and Observers. The two Parties may consider the possibility of replacing the arrangements hereby established with alternative arrangements by mutual agreement.

2. The provisions of the Treaty which relate to the establishment and functions and responsabilities of the UN Forces and Observers shall apply mutatis mutandis to the establishment and fuctions and responsabilities of the MFO or as provided in this Protocol.

3. The provisions of Article IV of the Treaty and the Agreed Minute thereto shall apply to the MFO. In accordance with paragraph 2 of this Protocol, the words "through the procedures indicated in paragraph 4 of Article IV and the Agreed Minute thereto" shall be substituted for "by the Security Council of the United Nations with the affirmative vote of the five permanent members" in paragraph 2 of Article IV of the Treaty.

4. The Parties shall agree on the nations from which the MFO will be drawn.

5. The mission of the MFO shall be to undertake the fuctions and responsibilities stipulated in the Treaty for the United Nations Forces and Observers. Details relating to the international nature, size, structure and operation of the MFO are set out in the attached Annex.

6. The Parties shall appoint a Director-General who shall be responsible for the direction of the MFO. The Director-General shall, subject to the approval of the Parties, appoint a Commander, who shall be responsible for the daily command of the MFO. Details relating to the Director-General and the Commander are set out in the attached Annex.

7. The expenses of the MFO which are not covered by other sources shall be borne equally by the parties.

8. Disputes arising from the interpretation and application of this Protocol shall be resolved according to Article VII of the Treaty.

9. This Protocol shall enter into force when each Party has notified the other that all its constitutional requirements have been fulfilled. The attached Annex shall be regarded as an integral part hereof. This Protocol shall be communicated to the Secretary General of the United Nations for registration in accordance with the provisions of Article 102 of the Charter of the United Nations.

(signed in Washington, D.C., August 3, 1981)

For the Government of the
Arab Republic of Egypt:

s/Ashraf A. Ghorbal

For the Government
of the State of Israel:

s/Efraim Evron

Witnessed by:

s/Alexander M. Haig Jr.

For the Government of the
United States of America

ANNEX

Director-General

1. The Parties shall appoint a Director-General of the MFO within one month of the signing of this Protocol. The Director-General shall serve a term of four years, which may be renewed. The Parties may replace the Director-General prior to the expiration of his term.

2. The Director-General shall be responsible for the direction of the MFO in the fulfillment of its functions and in this respect is authorized to act on behalf of the MFO. In accordance with local laws and regulations and the privileges and immunities of the MFO, the Director-General is authorized to engage an adequate staff, to institute legal proceedings, to contract, to acquire and dispose of property, and to take those other actions necessary and proper for the fulfillment of his responsabilities. The MFO shall not own immovable property in the territory of either Party without the agreement of the respective government. The Director-General shall determine the location of his office, subject to the consent of the country in which the office will be located.

3. Subject to the authorization of the Parties, the Director-General shall request those nations agreeable to the Parties to supply contingents to the MFO and to receive the agreement of contributing nations that the contingents will conduct themselves in accordance with the terms of this Protocol. The Director-General shall impress upon contributing nations the importance of continuity of service in units with the MFO so that the Commander may be in a position to plan his operations with knowledge of what units will be available. The Director-General shall obtain the agreement of contributing nations that the national contingents shall not be withdrawn without adequate prior notification to the Director-General.

4. The Director-General shall report to the Parties on developments relating to the functioning of the MFO. He may raise with either or both Parties, as appropriate, any matter concerning the functioning of the MFO. For this purpose, Egypt and Israel shall designate senior responsible officials as agreed points of contact for the Director-General. In the event that either Party or the Director-General requests a meeting, it will be convened in the location determined by the Director-General within 48 hours. Access across the international boundary shall only be permitted through entry checkpoints designated by each party. Such access will be in accordance with the laws and regulations of each country. Adequate procedures will be established by each Party to facilitate such entries.

Military Command Structure

5. In accordance with paragraph 6 of the Protocol, the Director-General shall appoint a Commander of the MFO within one month of the appointment of the Director-General. The Commander will be an officer of general rank and shall serve a term of three years which may, with the approval of the Parties, be renewed or curtailed. He shall not be of the same nationality as the Director-General.

6. Subject to paragraph 2 of this Annex, the Commander shall have full command authority over the MFO, and shall promulgate its Standing Operating Procedures. In making the command arrangements stipulated in paragraph 9 of Article VI of Annex I of the Treaty (hereinafter "Annex I"), the Commander shall establish a chain of command for the MFO linked to the commanders of the national contingents made available by contributing nations. The members of the MFO, although remaining in their national service, are, during the period of their assignment to the MFO, under the Director-General and subject to the authority of the Commander through the chain of command.

7. The Commander shall also have general responsibility for the good order of the MFO. Responsibility for disciplinary action in nation contingents provided for the MFO rests with the commanders of the national contingents.

Functions and Responsibilities of the MFO

8. The mission of the MFO shall be to undertake the functions and responsibilities stipulated in the Treaty for the United Nations Forces and Observers.

9. The MFO shall supervise the implementation of Annex I and employ its best efforts to prevent any violation of its terms.

10. With respect to the MFO, as appropriate, the Parties agree to the following arrangements:

(a) Operation of checkpoints, reconnaisance patrols, and observation posts along the international boundary and Line B, and within Zone C.

(b) Periodic verification of the implementation of the provisions of Annex I will be carried out not less than twice a month unless otherwise agreed by the Parties.

(c) Additional verifications within 48 hours after the receipt of a request from either Party.

(d) Ensuring the freedom of navigation through the Strait of Tiran in accordance with Article V of the Treaty of Peace.

11. When a violation has been confirmed by the MFO, it shall be rectified by the respective Party within 48 hours. The Party shall notify the MFO of the rectification.

12. The operations of the MFO shall not be construed as substituting for the undertaking by the Parties described in paragraph 2 of Article III of the Treaty. MFO personnel will report such acts by individuals as described in that paragraph in the first instance to the police of the respective Party.

13. Pursuant to paragraph 2 of Article II of Annex I, and in accordance with paragraph 7 of Article VI of Annex I, at the checkpoints at the international boundary, normal border crossing functions , such as passport inspection and customs control, will be carried out by officials of the respective Party.

14. The MFO operating in the Zones will enjoy freedom of movement necessary for the performance of its tasks.

15. MFO support flights to Egypt or Israel will follow normal rules and procedures for international flights. Egypt and Israel will undertake to facilitate clearances for such flights.

16. Verification flights by MFO aircraft in the Zones will be cleared with the authorities of the respective Party, in accordance with procedures to ensure that the flights can be undertaken in a timely manner.

17. MFO aircraft will not cross the international boundary without prior notification and clearance by each of the Parties.

18. MFO reconnaissance aircraft operating in Zone C will provide notification to the civil air control center and, thereby, to the Egyptian liaison officer therein.

Size and Organization

19. The MFO shall consist of a headquarters, three infantry battalions totalling not more than 2,000 troops, a coastal patrol unit and an observer unit, an aviation element and logistics and signal units.

20. The MFO units will have standard armament and equipment appropriate to their peacekeeping mission as stipulated in this Annex.

21. The MFO headquarters will be organized to fulfill its duties in accordance with the Treaty and this Annex. It shall be manned by staff-trained officers of appropriate rank provided by the troop contributing nations as part of their national contingents. Its organization will be determined by the Commander, who will assign staff positions to each contributor on an equitable basis.

Reports

22. The Commander will report findings simultaneously to the Parties as soon as possible, but not later than 24 hours, after a verification or after a violation has been confirmed. The Commander will also provide the Parties simultaneously a monthly report summarizing the findings of the checkpoints, observation posts, and reconnaissance patrols.

23. Reporting formats will be worked out by the Commander with the Parties in the Joint Commission. Reports to the Parties will be transmitted to the liaison offices to be established in accordance with paragraph 31 below.

Financing, Administration and Facilities

24. The budget for each financial year shall be prepared by the Director-General and shall be approved by the Parties. The financial year shall be from October 1 through September 30. Contributions shall be paid in U.S. dollars, unless the Director-General requests contributions in some other form. Contributions shall be committed the first day of the financial year and made available as the Director-General determines necessary to meet expenditures of the MFO.

25. For the period prior to October 1, 1981, the budget of the MFO shall consist of such sums as the Director-General shall receive. Any contributions during that period will be credited to the share of the budget of the contributing state in Financial Year 1982, and thereafter as necessary, so that the contribution is fully credited.

26. The Director-General shall prepare financial and administrative regulations consistent with this Protocol and submit them no later than December 1, 1981, for the approval of the Parties. These financial regulations shall include a budgetary process which takes into

account the budgetary cycles of the contributing states.

27. The Commander shall request the approval of the respective Party for the use of facilities on its territory necessary for the proper functioning of the MFO. In this connection, the respective Party, after giving its approval for the use by the MFO of land or existing buildings and their fixtures, will not be reimbursed by the MFO for such use.

Responsibilities of the Joint Commission Prior to Its Dissolution

28. In accordance with Article IV of the Appendix to Annex I, the Joint Commission will supervise the implementation of the arrangements described in Annex I and its Appendix, as indicated in subparagraphs b, c, h, i and j of paragraph 3 of Article IV.

29. The Joint Commission will implement the preparations required to enable the Liaison System to undertake its responsibilities in accordance with Article VII of Annex I.

30. The Joint Commission will determine the modalities and procedures for the implementation of Phase Two, as described in paragraph 3 (b) of Article I of Annex I, based on the modalities and procedures that were implemented in Phase One.

Liaison System

31. The Liaison System will undertake the responsibilities indicated in paragraph 1 of Article VII of Annex I, and may discuss any other matters which the Parties by agreement may place before it. Meetings will be held at least once a month. In the event that either Party or the Commander requests a special meeting, it will be convened within 24 hours. The first meeting will be held in El Arish not later than two weeks after the MFO assumes its functions. Meetings will alternate between El Arish and Beer-Sheba, unless the Parties otherwise agree. The Commander shall be invited to any meeting in which subjects concerning the MFO are discussed, or when either Party requests MFO presence. Decisions will be reached by agreement of Egypt and Israel.

32. The Commander and each chief liaison officer will have access to one another in their respective offices. Adequate procedures will be worked out between the Parties with a view to facilitating the entry for this purpose of the representatives of either Party to the territory of the other.

Privileges and Immunities

33. Each Party will accord to the MFO the privileges and immunities indicated in the attached Appendix.

Schedule

34. The MFO shall assume its functions at 1300 hours on April 25, 1982.

35. The MFO shall be in place by 1300 hours, on March 20, 1982.

APPENDIX

Definitions

1. The "Multinational Force and Observers" (hereinafter referred to as "the MFO") is that organization established by the Protocol.

2. For the purposes of this Appendix, the term "Member of the MFO" refers to the Director-General, the Commander and any person, other than a resident of the Receiving State, belonging to the military contingent of a Participating State or otherwise under the authority of the Director-General, and his spouse and minor children, as appropriate.

3. The "Receiving State" means the authorities of Egypt or Israel as appropriate, and the territories under their control. "Government authorities" includes all national and local, civil and military authorities called upon to perform functions relating to the MFO under the provisions of this Appendix, without prejudice to the ultimate responsibility of the Government of the Receiving State.

4. "Resident of the Receiving State" includes (a) a person with citizenship of the Receiving State, (b) a person resident therein or (c) a person present in the territory of the Receiving State other than a member of the MFO.

5. "Participating State" means a State that contributes personnel to the MFO.

Duties of members of the MFO in the Receiving State:

6. (a) Members of the MFO shall respect the laws and regulations of the Receiving State and shall refrain from any activity of a political character in the Receiving State and from any action incompatible with the international nature of their duties or inconsistent with the spirit of the present arrangements. The Director-General shall take all appropriate measures to ensure the observance of these obligations.

(b) In the performance of their duties for the MFO, members of the MFO shall receive their instructions only from the Director-General and the chain of command designated by him.

(c) Members of the MFO shall exercise the utmost discretion in regard to all matters relating to their duties and functions. They shall not communicate to any person any information known to them by reason of their position with the MFO which has not been made public, except in the course of their duties or by authorization of the Director-General. These obligations do not cease upon the termination of their assignment with the MFO.

(d) The Director-General will ensure that in the Standing Operating Procedures of the MFO, there will be arrangements to avoid accidental or inadvertent threats to the safety of MFO members.

Entry and exit: Identification

7. Individual or collective passports shall be issued by the Participating States for members of the MFO. The Director-General shall notify the Receiving State of the names and scheduled time of arrival of MFO members, and other necessary information. The Receiving State shall issue an individual or collective multiple-entry visa as appropriate prior to that travel. No other documents shall be required for a member of the MFO to enter or leave the Receiving State. Members of the MFO shall be exempt from immigration inspection and restrictions on entering or departing from the territory of the Receiving State. They shall also be exempt from any regulations governing the residence of aliens in the Receiving State, including registration, but shall not be considered as acquiring any right to permanent residence or domicile in the Receiving State. The Receiving State shall also provide each member of the Force with a personal identity card prior to or upon his arrival.

8. Members of the MFO will at all times carry their personal identity cards issued by the Receiving State. Members of the MFO may be required to present, but not to surrender, their passport or identity cards upon demand of an appropriate authority of the Receiving State. Except as provided in paragraph 7 of this Appendix, the passport or identity card will be the only document required for a member of the MFO.

9. If a member of the MFO leaves the services of the Participating State to which he belongs and is not repatriated, the Director-General shall immediately inform the authorities of the Receiving State, giving such particulars as may be required. The Director-General shall similarly inform the authorities of the Receiving State of any member of the MFO who has absented himself for more than twenty-one days. If an expulsion order against the ex-member of the MFO has been made, the Director-General shall be responsible for ensuring that the person concerned shall be received within the territory of the Participating State concerned.

Jurisdiction

10. The following arrangements respecting criminal and civil jurisdiction are made having regard to the special functions of the MFO and not for the personal benefit of the members of the MFO. The Director-General shall cooperate at all times with the appropriate authorities of the Receiving State to facilitate the proper administration of justice, secure the observance of laws and regulations and prevent the occurrence of any abuse in connection with the privileges, immunities and facilities mentioned in this Appendix.

Criminal jurisdiction

11. (a) Military members of the MFO and members of the civilian observer group of the MFO shall be subject to the exclusive jurisdiction of their respective national states in respect of any criminal offenses which may be committed by them in the Receiving State. Any such person who is charged with the commission of a crime will be brought to trial by the respective Participating State, in accordance with its laws.

(b) Subject to paragraph 25, other members of the MFO shall be immune from the criminal jurisdiction of the Receiving State in respect of words spoken or written and all acts performed by them in their official capacity.

(c) The Director-General shall obtain the assurances of each Participating State that it will be prepared to take the necessary measures to assure proper discipline of its personnel and to exercise jurisdiction with respect to any crime or offense which might be committed by its personnel. The Director-General shall comply with requests of the Receiving State for the withdrawal from its territory of any member of the MFO who violates its laws, regulations, customs or traditions. The Director-General, with the consent of the Participating State, may waive the immunity of a member of the MFO.

(d) Without prejudice to the foregoing, a Participating State may enter into a supplementary arrangement with the Receiving State to limit or waive the immunities of its members of the MFO who are on periods of leave while in the Receiving State.

Civil jurisdiction

12. (a) Members of the MFO shall not be subject to the civil jurisdiction of the courts of the Receiving State or to other legal process in any matter relating to their official duties. In a case arising from a matter relating to official duties and which involves a member of the MFO and a resident of the Receiving State, and in other disputes as agreed, the procedure provided in paragraph 38 (b) of this Appendix shall apply to the settlement.

(b) If the Director-General certifies that a member of the MFO is unable because of official duties or authorized absence to protect his interests in a civil proceeding in which he is a participant, the court or authority shall at his request suspend the proceeding until the elimination of the disability, but for not more than ninety days. Property of a member of the MFO which is certified by the Director-General to be needed by him for the fulfillment of his official duties shall be free from seizure for the satisfaction of a judgment, decision or order, together with other property not subject thereto under the law of the Receiving State. The personal liberty of a member of the MFO shall not be restricted by a court or other authority of the Receiving State in a civil proceeding, whether to enforce a judgment, decision or order, to compel an oath of diclosure, or for any other reason.

(c) In the cases provided for in sub-paragraph (b) above, the claimant may elect to have his claim dealt with in accordance with the procedure set out in paragraph 38 (b) of this Appendix. Where a claim adjudicated or an award made in favor of the claimant by a court of the Receiving State or the Claims Commission under paragraph 38 (b) of this Appendix has not been satisfied, the authorities of the Receiving State may, without prejudice to the claimant's rights, seek the good offices of the Director-General to obtain satisfaction.

Notification: certification

13. If any civil proceeding is instituted against a member of the MFO, before any court of the Receiving State having jurisdiction, notification shall be given to the Director-General. The Director-General shall certify to the court whether or not the proceeding is related to the official duties of such member.

Military police: arrest: transfer of custody and mutual assistance

14. The Director-General shall take all appropriate measures to ensure maintenance of discipline and good order among members of the MFO. To this end military police designated by the Director-General shall police the premises referred to in paragraph 19 of this Appendix, and such areas where the MFO is functioning.

15. The military police of the MFO shall immediately transfer to the civilian police of the Receiving State any individual, who is not a member of the MFO, of whom it takes temporary custody.

16. The police of the Receiving State shall immediately transfer to the MFO any member of the MFO, of whom it takes temporary custody, pending a determination concerning jurisdiction.

17. The Director-General and the authorities of the Receiving State shall assist each other concerning all offenses in respect of which either or both have an interest, including the production of witnesses, and in the collection and production of evidence, including the seizure and, in proper cases, the handing over of any such things may be made subject to their return within the time specified by the authority delivering them. Each shall notify the other of the disposition of any case in the outcome of which the other may have an interest or in which there has been a transfer of custody under the provisions of paragraphs 15 and 16 of this Appendix.

18. The government of the Receiving State will ensure the prosecution of persons subject to its criminal jurisdiction who are accused of acts in relation to the MFO or its members which, if committed in relation to the forces of the receiving State or their members, would have rendered them liable to prosecution. The Director-General will take the measures within his power with respect to crimes or offenses committed against citizens of the Receiving State by members of the MFO.

Premises of the MFO

19. Without prejudice to the fact that all the premises of the MFO remain the territory of the Receiving State, they shall be inviolable and subject to the exclusive control and authority of the Director-General, who alone may consent to the entry of officials to perform duties on such premises.

MFO flag

20. The Receiving States permit the MFO to display a special flag or insignia, of a design agreed upon by them, on its headquarters, camps, posts, or other premises, vehicles, boats and otherwise as decided by the Director-General. Other flags or pennants may be displayed only in exceptional cases and in accordance with conditions prescribed by the Director-General. Sympathetic consideration will be given to observations or requests of the authorities of the Receiving State concerning this last-mentioned matter. If the MFO flag or other flag is flown, the flag of the Receiving State shall be flown alongside it.

Uniform: Vehicle, boat and aircraft markings and registration: Operating permits

21. Military members of the MFO shall normally wear their national uniform with such identifying MFO insignia as the Director-Genral may prescribe.
The conditions on which the wearing of civilian dress is authorized shall be notified by the Director-General to the authorities of the Receiving State and sympathetic consideration will be given to observations or requests of the authorities of the Receiving State concerning this matter. Members of the MFO shall wear civilian dress while outside the area where they are functioning. Service vehicles, boats and aircraft shall not carry the marks or license plates of any Participating State, but shall carry the distinctive MFO identification mark and license which shall be notified by the Director-General to the authorities of the Receiving State. Such vehicles, boats and aircraft shall not be subject to registration and licensing under the laws and regulations of the Receiving State. Authorities of the Receiving State shall accept as valid, without a test or fee, a permit or license for the operation of service vehicles, boats and aircraft issued by the Director-General. MFO drivers shall be given permits by the Receiving State to enable them to drive outside the areas where they are functioning, if these permits are required by the Receiving State.

Arms

22. Members of the MFO who are off-duty shall not carry arms while outside the areas where they are functioning.

Privileges and immunities of the MFO

23. The MFO shall enjoy the status, privileges and immunities accorded in Article II of the Convention on the Privileges and Immunities of the United Nations (hereinafter, "the Convention"). The provisions of Article II of the Convention shall also apply to the property, funds and assets of Participating States used in the Receiving State in connection with the activities of the MFO. Such Participating States may not acquire immovable property in the Receiving State without agreement of the government of the Receiving State. The government of the Receiving State recognizes that the right of the MFO to import free-of-duty equipment for the MFO and provisions, supplies and other goods for the exclusive use of members of the MFO, includes the right of the MFO to establish, maintain and operate at headquarters camps and posts, service institutes providing amenities for the members of the MFO. The amenities that may be provided by service institutes shall be goods of a consumable nature (tobacco and tobacco products, beer, etc.), and other customary articles of small value. To the end that duty-free importation for the MFO may be effected with the least possible delay, having regard to the interests of the government of the Receiving State, a mutually satisfactory procedure, including documentation, shall be arranged between the Director-General and the customs authorities of the Receiving State. The Director-General shall take all necessary measures to prevent any abuse of the exemption and to prevent the sale or resale of such goods to persons other than the members of the MFO. Sympathetic consideration shall be given by the Director-General to observations or requests of the authorities of the Receiving State concerning the operation of service institutes.

Privileges and immunities and delegation of authority of Director-General

24. The Director-General of the MFO may delegate his powers to other members of the MFO.

25. The Director-General, his deputy, the Commander, and his deputy, shall be accorded in respect of themselves, their spouses and minor children, the privileges and immunities,

exemptions and facilities accorded to diplomatic envoys in accordance with international law.

Members of the MFO: Taxation, customs and fiscal regulations

26. Members of the MFO shall be exempt from taxation by the Receiving State on the pay and emoluments received from their national governments or from the MFO. They shall also be exempt from all other direct taxes, fees and charges except for those levied for services rendered.

27. Members of the MFO shall have the right to import free of duty their personal effects in connection with their first taking up their post in the Receiving State. They shall be subject to the laws and regulations of the Receiving State governing customs and foreign exchange with respect to personal property not required by them by reason of their presence in the Receiving State with the MFO. Special facilities for entry or exit shall be granted by the immigration, customs and fiscal authorities of the Receiving State to regularly constituted units of the MFO provided that the authorities concerned have been duly notified sufficiently in advance. Members of the MFO on departure from the area may, notwithstanding the foreign exchange regulations, take with them such funds as the Director-General certifies were received in pay and emoluments from their respective national governments or from the MFO and are a reasonable residue thereof. Special arrangements between the Director-General and the authorities of the Receiving State shall be made for the implementation of the foregoing provisions in the interests of the government of the Receiving State and members of the MFO.

28. The Director-General will cooperate with the customs and fiscal authorities of the Receiving State and will render all assistance within his power in ensuring the observance of the customs and fiscal laws and regulations of the Receiving State by the members of the MFO in accordance with this Appendix or any relevant supplemental arrangements.

Communications and postal services

29. The MFO shall enjoy the facilities in respect to communications provided for in Article III of the Convention. The Director-General shall have authority to install and operate communications systems as are necessary to perform its functions subjects to the provisions of Article 35 of the International Telecommunications Convention of April 11, 1973, relating to harmful interference. The frequencies on which any such station may be operate will be duly communicated by the MFO to the appropriate authorities of the Receiving State. Appropriate consultations will be held between the MFO and the authorities of the Receiving State to avoid harmful interference. The right of the Director-General is likewise recognized to enjoy the priorities of government telegrams and telephone calls as provided for the United Nations in Article 39 and Annex 3 of the latter Convention and in Article 5, No. 10 of the telegraph regulations annexed thereto.

30. The MFO shall also enjoy, within the areas where it is functioning, the right of unrestricted communication by radio, telephone, telegraph or any other means, and of establishing the necessary facilities for maintaining such communications within and between premises of the MFO, including the laying of cables and land lines and the establishment of fixed and mobile radio sending and receiving stations. It is understood that the telegraph and telephone cables and lines herein referred to will be situated within or directly between the premises of the MFO and the areas where it is functioning, and that connection with the system of telegraphs and telephones of the Receiving State will be made in accordance with arrangements with the appropriate authorities of the Receiving State.

31. The government of the Receiving State recognizes the right of the MFO to make arrangements through its own facilities for the processing and transport of private mail addressed to or emanating from members of the MFO. The government of the Receiving State will be informed of the nature of such arrangements. No interference shall take place with, and no censorship shall be applied to the mail of the MFO by the government of the Receiving State. In the event that postal arrangements applying to private mail of members of the MFO are extended to operations involving transfer of currency, or transport of packages or parcels from the Receiving State, the conditions under which such operations shall be conducted in the Receiving State will be agreed upon between the government of the Receiving State and the Director-General.

Motor vehicle insurance

32. The MFO will take necessary arrangements to ensure that all MFO motor vehicles shall be covered by third party liability insurance in accordance with the laws and regulations of the Receiving State.

Use of roads, waterways, port facilities, airfields and railways

33. When the MFO uses roads, bridges, port facilities and airfields it shall not be subject to payment of dues, tolls or charges either by way of registration or otherwise, in the areas where it is functioning and the normal points of access, except for charges that are related directly to services rendered. The authorities of the Receiving State, subject to special arrangements, will give the most favorable consideration to requests for the grant to members of the MFO of traveling facilities on its railways and of concessions with regard to fares.

Water, electricity and other public utilities

34. The MFO shall have the right to the use of water, electricity and other public utilities at rates no less favorable to the MFO than those to comparable consumers. The authorities of the Receiving State will, upon the request of the Director-General, assist the MFO in obtaining water, electricity and other utilities required, and in the case of interruption or threatened interruption of service, will give the same priority to the needs of the MFO as to essential government services. The MFO shall have the right where necessary to generate, within the premises of the MFO either on land or water, electricity for the use of the MFO and to transmit and distribute such electricity as required by the MFO.

Currency of the Receiving State

35. The Government of the Receiving State will, if requested by the Director-General, make available to the MFO, against reimbursement in U.S. dollars or other currency mutually acceptable, currency of the Receiving State required for the use of the MFO, including the pay of the members of the national contingents, at the rate of exchange most favorable to the MFO that is officially recognized by the government of the Receiving State.

Provisions, supplies and services

36. The authorities of the Receiving State will, upon the request of the Director-General, assist the MFO in obtaining equipment, provisions, supplies and other goods and services required from local sources for its subsistence and operation. Sympathetic consideration will be given by the Director-General in purchases on the local market to requests or observations of the authorities of the Receiving State in order to

avoid any adverse effect on the local economy. Members of the MFO may purchase locally goods necessary for their own consumption, and such services as they need, under conditions prevailing in the open market.

If members of the MFO should require medical or dental facilities beyond those available within the MFO, arrangements shall be made with the appropriate authorities of the Receiving State under which such facilities may be made available. The Director-General and the appropriate local authorities will cooperate with respect to sanitary services. The Director-General and the authorities of the Receiving State shall extend to each other the fullest cooperation in matters concerning health, particularly with respect to the control of communicable diseases in accordance with international conventions; such cooperation shall extend to the exchange of relevant information and statistics.

Locally recruited personnel

37. The MFO may recruit locally such personnel as required. The authorities of the Receiving State will, upon the request of the Director-General, assist the MFO in the recruitment of such personnel. Sympathetic consideration will be given by the Director-General in the recruitment of local personnel to requests or observations of authorities of the Receiving State in order to avoid any adverse effect on the local economy. The terms and conditions of employment for locally recruited personnel shall be prescribed by the Director-General and shall generally, to the extent practicable, be no less favorable than the practice prevailing in the Receiving State.

Settlement of disputes or claims

38. Disputes or claims of a private law character shall be settled in accordance with the following provisions:

a) The MFO shall make provisions for the appropriate modes of settlement of disputes or claims arising out of contract or other disputes or claims of a private law character to which the MFO is a party other than those covered in subparagraph (b) and paragraph 39 following. When no such provisions have been made with the contracting party, such claims shall be settled according to subparagraph (b) below.
b) Any claim made by:
   i) a resident of the Receiving State against the MFO or a member thereof, in respect of any damages alleged to result from an act of omission of such member or the

MFO relating to his official duties;

ii) the Government of the Receiving State against a member of the MFO;

iii) the MFO or the Government of the Receiving State against one another, that is not covered by paragraph 40 of this Appendix;

shall be settled by a Claims Commission established for that purpose. One member of the Commission shall be appointed by the Director-General, one member by the Government of the Receiving State and a Chairman jointly by the two. If the Director-General and the Government of the Receiving State fail to agree on the appointment of a chairman, the two members selected by them shall select a chairman from the list of the Permanent Court of Arbitration. An award made by the Claims Commission against the MFO or a member or other employee thereof or against the Government of the Receiving State shall be notified to the Director-General or the authorities of the Receiving State as the case may be, to make satisfaction thereof.

39. Disputes concerning the terms of employment and conditions of services of locally recruited personnel shall be settled by administrative procedure to be established by the Director-General.

40. All disputes between the MFO and the Government of the Receiving State concerning the interpretation or application of this Appendix which are not settled by negotiation or other agreed mode of settlement shall be referred for final settlement to a tribunal of three arbitrators, one to be named by the Director-General, one by the Government of the Receiving State, and an umpire to be chosen jointly who shall preside over the proceedings of this tribunal.

41. If the two parties fail to agree on the appointment of the umpire within one month of the proposal of arbitration by one of the parties, the two members selected by them shall select a chairman from the list of the Permanent Court of Arbitration. Should a vacancy occur for any reason, the vacancy shall be filled within thirty days by the methods laid down in this paragraph for the original appointment. The tribunal shall come into existence upon the appointment of the chairman and at least one of the other members of the tribunal. Two members of the tribunal shall constitute a quorum for the performance of its functions, and for all deliberations and decisions of the tribunal a favorable vote of two members shall be sufficient.

Deceased members: disposition of personal property

42. The Director-General shall have the right to take charge of and dispose of the body of a member of the MFO who dies in the territory of the Receiving State and may dispose of his personal property after the debts of the deceased person incurred in the territory of the Receiving State and owing to residents of the Receiving State have been settled.

Supplemental arrangements

43. Supplemental details for the carrying out of this Appendix shall be made as required between the Director-General and appropriate authorities designated by the Government of the Receiving State.

Effective date and duration

44. This Appendix shall take effect from the date of the entry into force of the Protocol and shall remain in force for the duration of the Protocol. The provisions of paragraphs 38, 39, 40 and 41 of this Appendix, relating to the settlement of disputes, however, shall remain in force until all claims arising prior to the date of termination of this Appendix and submitted prior to or within three months following the date of termination, have been settled.

Appendix D
Exchanges of Letters

**LETTERS FROM PRESIDENT CARTER
TO PRESIDENT SADAT AND PRIME MINISTER
BEGIN**

March 26, 1979

Dear Mr. President:

I wish to confirm to you that subject to United States Constitutional processes:

In the event of an actual or threatened violation of the Treaty of Peace between Egypt and Israel, the United States will, on request of one or both of the Parties, consult with the Parties with respect thereto and will take such other action as it may deem appropriate and helpful to achieve compliance with the Treaty.

The United States will conduct aerial monitoring as requested by the Parties pursuant to Annex I of the Treaty.

The United States believes the Treaty provision for permanent stationing of United Nations personnel in the designed limited force zone can and should be implemented by the United Nations Security Council. The United States will exert its utmost efforts to obtain the requisite action by the Security Council. If the Security Council fails to establish and maintain the arrangements called for in the Treaty, the President will be prepared to take those steps necessary to ensure the establishment and maintenance of an acceptable alternative multinational force.

Sincerely,

Jimmy Carter

His Excellency
  Mohamed Anwar El-Sadat,
    President of the Arab
    Republic of Egypt.

March 26, 1979

Dear Mr. Prime Minister:

I wish to confirm to you that subject to United States Constitutional processes:

In the event of an actual or threatened violation of the Treaty of Peace between Israel and Egypt, the United States will, on request of one or both of the Parties, consult with the Parties with respect thereto and will take such other action as it may deem appropriate and helpful to achieve compliance with the Treaty.

The United States will conduct aerial monitoring as requested by the Parties pursuant to Annex I of the Treaty.

The United States believes the Treaty provision for permanent stationing of United Nations personnel in the designed limited force zone can and should be implemented by the United Nations Security Council. The United States will exert its utmost efforts to obtain the requisite action by the Security Council. If the Security Council fails to establish and maintain the arrangements called for in the Treaty, the President will be prepared to take those steps necessary to ensure the establishment and maintenance of an acceptable alternative multinational force.

Sincerely,

Jimmy Carter

His Excellency
  Menachem Begin,
    Prime Minister of the
    State of Israel.

**EXCHANGE OF LETTERS BETWEEN
SECRETARY OF STATE HAIG AND FOREIGN
AFFAIRS MINISTERS ALI AND SHAMIR**

August 3, 1981

Dear Mr. Minister:

I wish to confirm the understandings concerning the United States' role reached in your negotiations on the establishment and maintenance of the Multinational Force and Observers:

1. The post of the Director-General will be held by U.S. nationals suggested by the United States.
2. Egypt and Israel will accept proposals made by the United States concerning the appointment of the Director-General, the appointment of the Commander, and the financial issues related to paragraphs 24-26 of the Annex to the Protocol, if no agreement is reached on any of these issues between the Parties. The United States will participate in deliberations concerning finˑncial matters. In the event of differences of view between the Parties over the composition of the MFO, the two sides will invite the United States to join them in resolving any issues.
3. Subject to Congressional authorization and appropriations:

   A. The United States will contribute an · infantry battalion and a logistics support unit from its armed forces and will provide a group of civilian observers to the MFO.
   B. The United States will contribute one-third of the annual operating expenses of the MFO. The United States will be reimbursed by the MFO for the costs

incurred in the change of station of U.S. Armed Forces provided to the MFO and for the costs incurred in providing civilian observers to the MFO. For the initial period (July 17, 1981 - September 30, 1982) during which there will be exceptional costs connected with the establishment of the MFO, the United States agrees to provide three-fifths of the costs, subject to the same understanding concerning reimbursement.

   C. The United States will use its best efforts to find acceptable replacements for contingents that withdraw from the MFO.
   D. The United States remains prepared to take those steps necessary to ensure the maintenance of an acceptable MFO.

I wish to inform you that I sent today to the Minister of Foreign Affairs of Israel an identical letter, and I propose that my letters and the replies thereto constitute an agreement among the three States.

Sincerely,

Alexander M. Haig, Jr.

His Excellency
  Kamal Hassan Ali,
  Deputy Prime Minister
    and Minister of Foreign Affairs,
    Egypt.

August 3, 1981

Dear Mr. Minister:

I wish to confirm the understandings concerning the United States' role reached in your negotiations on the establishment and maintenance of the Multinational Force and Observers:

1. The post of the Director-General will be held by U.S. nationals suggested by the United States.

2. Egypt and Israel will accept proposals made by the United States concerning the appointment of the Commander, and the financial issues related to paragraphs 24-26 of the Annex to the Protocol, if no agreement is reached on any of these issues between the Parties. The United States will participate in deliberations concerning financial matters. In the event of differences of view between the parties over the composition of the MFO, the two sides will invite the U.S. to join them in resolving any issues.

3. Subject to Congressional authorization and appropriations:

A. The United States will contribute an infantry battalion and a logistics support unit from its armed forces and will provide a group of civilian observers to the MFO.

B. The United States will contribute one-third of the annual operating expenses of the MFO. The United States will be reimbursed by the MFO for the costs incurred in the change of station of U.S. Armed Forces provided to the MFO and for the costs incurred in providing civilian observers to the MFO. For the initial period (July 1, 1981 - September 30, 1982) during which there will be exceptional costs connected with the establishment of the MFO, the United States agrees to provide three-fifths of the costs, subjects to the same understanding concerning reimbursement.

C. The United States will use its best efforts to find acceptable replacements for contingents that withdraw from the MFO.

D. The United States remains prepared to take those ste s necessary to ensure the maintenance of an acceptable MFO.

I wish to inform you that I sent today to the Minister of Foreign Affairs of Egypt an identical letter, and I propose that my letters and the replies thereto constitute an agreement among the three States.

Sincerely

Alexander M. Haig, Jr

His Excellency
Yitzhak Shamir
Foreign Minister
Israel

162

August 3, 1981

3 August 1981

The Honorable
Alexander M. Haig, Jr.
Secretary of State
Washington, D.C.

The Honorable
Alexander M. Haig, Jr.
Secretary of State
Washington, D.C.

Dear Mr. Secretary:

I am instructed on behalf of Foreign Minister
Ali to transmit the following letter:

Sincerely,

Ashraf A. Ghorbal
Ambassador

Dear Mr. Secretary,

I have been asked by Foreign Minister Shamir
to transmit to you the following message:

"Dear Mr. Secretary:

Israel agrees to the contents of your letter
dated August 3, 1981 and wishes to express its
appreciation to the United States for having
helped the two countries to reach this
agreement.

Dear Mr. Secretary:

Egypt agrees to the contents of your letter
dated August 3, 1981, and wishes to express its
appreciation to the United States for having
helped the two countries to reach this
agreement.

Sincerely,

Kamal Hassan Ali
Deputy Prime Minister
Minister of Foreign Affairs

Sincerely,

(sgd)
Yitzhak Shamir
Foreign
Minister"

Sincerely,

Ephraim Evron
Ambassador

Appendix E
MFO Financial Statements

OFFICE OF GOVERNMENT SERVICES

1801 K STREET, N.W.
WASHINGTON, DC 20006
202 296-0800

November 9, 1983

Director General
Multinational Force
and Observers

In our opinion, the accompanying balance sheet and related statements of revenues, expenses and changes in unrestricted net assets and of changes in financial position present fairly the financial position of Multinational Force and Observers at September 30, 1983 and 1982, and the results of its operations and the changes in its financial position for the year ended September 30, 1983 and for the period September 9, 1981 (inception) to September 30, 1982 in conformity with generally accepted accounting principles consistently applied. Our examinations of these statements were made in accordance with generally accepted auditing standards and accordingly included such tests of the accounting records and such other auditing procedures as we considered necessary in the circumstances.

Price Waterhouse

BALANCE SHEET

ASSETS

	September 30,	
	1983	**1982**
Current assets		
Cash	$ 493,908	$ 6,768,360
Bank time deposits (Note 3)	6,200,000	2,000,000
Prepaid expenses and other receivables	2,157,815	1,444,162
Pledges (Note 2)	18,000,000	26,000,000
Loan to Force Exchange (Note 4)	400,000	–
Total current assets	27,251,723	36,212,522
Equipment, buildings and facilities (Note 2)	–	–
Loan to Force Exchange (Note 4)	400,000	–
Investment in Force Exchange (Note 4)	1,000,000	1,000,000
	$ 28,651,723	**$ 37,212,522**

LIABILITIES AND NET ASSETS

	1983	1982
Current liabilities		
Accounts payable	$ 825,413	$ 2,124,045
Accrued expenses	7,157,733	2,475,728
Deffered interest income (Note 5)	1,286,291	4,467,046
Total current liabilities	9,269,437	9,066,819
Net assets		
Reserved for encumbrances (Note 2)	5,658,146	12,664,763
Unrestricted	13,724,140	15,480,940
Total net assets	19,382,286	28,145,703
	$ 28,651,723	**$ 37,212,522**

See accompanying Notes to Financial Statements.

STATEMENT OF REVENUE, EXPENSES AND CHANGES IN UNRESTRICTED NET ASSETS FOR THE YEAR ENDED SEPTEMBER 30, 1983 AND FOR THE PERIOD SEPTEMBER 9, 1981 (INCEPTION) TO SEPTEMBER 30, 1982

	1983	1982
Revenue		
Support (Notes 1 and 2)		
Egypt	$ 31,397,686	$ 45,000,000
Israel	31,397,686	45,000,000
United States	25,171,674	135,000,000
Total revenue	87,967,046	225,000,000
Expenses		
Building and facilities (Note 2)	4,224,246	100,716,171
Communications	2,553,155	12,542,758
Contractual services	26,412,707	17,223,639
Equipment and furnishings (Note 2)	5,374,684	18,112,885
Personnel (Note 6)	22,168,931	12,771,781
Petroleum, oil and lubricants (Note 2)	6,322,462	4,302,984
Rents	945,923	602,988
Supplies, materials and services (Note 2)	16,729,771	16,675,007
Transportation	3,770,166	7,758,715
Travel	1,447,167	1,148,847
Troop rotation	6,399,743	4,858,073
Utilities	381,508	140,449
Total expenses	96,730,463	196,854,297
Excess (deficiency) of revenue over expenses	(8,763,417)	28,145,703
Amount reserved for encumbrances		
Beginning of period	12,664,763	–
End of period	(5,658,146)	(12,664,763)
Unrestricted net assets, beginning of period	15,480,940	–
Unrestricted net assets, end of period	**$ 13,724,140**	**$ 15,480,940**

See accompanying Notes to Financial Statements.

STATEMENT OF CHANGES IN FINANCIAL POSITION
FOR THE YEAR ENDED SEPTEMBER 30, 1983
AND FOR THE PERIOD SEPTEMBER 9, 1981 (INCEPTION)
TO SEPTEMBER 30, 1982

	1983	1982
Sources of cash		
Excess (deficit) of revenue over expenses	$ (8,763,417)	$ 28,145,703
Less revenue not providing cash in current period		
Pledges - net	(8,000,000)	26,000,000
Cash provided (used) by operations	(763,417)	2,145,703
Accounts payable and accrued expenses	3,383,373	4,599,773
Deferred interest income	(3,180,755)	4,467,046
Total sources (uses) of cash	(560,799)	11,212,522
Uses of cash		
Investment in Force Exchange	–	1,000,000
Advances to Force Exchange	800,000	–
Bank time deposits	4,200,000	2,000,000
Prepaid expenses and other eceivables	713,653	1,444,162
Total uses of cash	5,713,653	4,444,162
Cash, beginning of period	6,768,360	–
Cash, end of period	$ 493,908	$ 6,768,360

See accompanying Notes to Financial Statements.

MULTINATIONAL FORCE AND OBSERVERS

NOTES TO FINANCIAL STATEMENTS
SEPTEMBER 30, 1983

Note 1 – The Organization

The Multinational Force and Observers (MFO) is an international organization established by the Protocol signed by the Governments of Egypt and Israel (the Receiving States) and witnessed by the United States on August 3, 1981. The MFO's function is to supervise and implement key security provisions of the Treaty of Peace between Egypt and Israel dated March 26, 1979. The MFO received its initial funding on September 9, 1981.

Each of the Receiving States and the United States agreed to contribute equally to the annual operating expenses of the MFO except for the initial period, August 3, 1981 through September 30, 1982, when the United States provided three-fifths of the cost and Egypt and Israel each provided one-fifth of the cost.

Note 2 – Summary of Significant Accounting Policies

The financial statements of MFO are prepared on the accrual basis. The financial statements and the accounting principles on which they are based generally follow the recommendations of Statement of Position 78-10 «Accounting Principles and Reporting Practices for Certain Nonprofit Organizations» issued by the American Institute of Certified Public Accountants. The significant accounting policies followed are described below:

Revenue Recognition
All of the organization's revenues are derived from support contributions by the Receiving States and the United States. Support is recognized based on amounts pledged to MFO in accordance with the current financial year budget that are supported by collections or letters of credit.

Encumbrances
Encumbrances consist of commitments in the form of orders and contracts for supplies, materials, equipment and services, except for personal compensation and allowances, that will be delivered or rendered during the following year.

Buildings and Facilities
Cost of real estate improvements in the Sinai are charged to expense as incurred because MFO has no legal title to the improvements and the facilities.

Equipment and Furnishings
Costs of equipment and furnishings are charged to expense as incurred because it is most improbable that equipment and furnishings can be removed economically from the Sinai once delivered.

Supplies and Stores Inventory
Costs of supplies and stores items are charged to expense as they are received.

Foreign Exchange
Exchange adjustments arising from translation of foreign currencies are included in the results of operations currently.

Note 3 – Restricted Cash

In connection with certain contracts for the supply of oil, fuel and lubricant products, MFO has agreed to maintain a $1.2 million bank time deposit, due September 30, 1984, as security for a Letter of Guaranty for $1.2 million issued in favor of the vendor.

Note 4 – Force Exchange

The MFO operates, on a not-for-profit basis, a Force Exchange in the Sinai for the benefit of participating troops and civilian personnel. The MFO Force Exchange operations are distinct and autonomous from those of the MFO and are recorded in separate bank accounts and financial and accounting records. MFO has invested $1,000,000 to provide the basic working capital required by the MFO Force Exchange to maintain operating cash and inventory levels, and $800,000 to meet short term working capital requirements, of which $400,000 is repayable during the year ending September 30, 1984 and $400,000 is repayable during the year ending September 30, 1985.

Note 5 – Deferred Interest Income

The MFO Administrative and Financial Regulations required by the Protocol state that each year's interest income shall be applied as partial payment of the amount pledged by the Fund Contributing States in the following year.

Note 6 – Contributed Services

For troop contingents provided by developed nations, MFO reimburses the cost of special pay and allowances required by applicable national legislation for troops serving abroad. Equivalent costs of troops stationed at home are borne by the respective nations as contributions to the peacekeeping mission of the MFO. The value of these contributions is not reflected in these statements.

Abbreviations

ANZAC	Australia-New Zealand Army Corps
BOR	Buffer Observation and Reconnaissance
COU	Civilian Observer Unit
CP	Checkpoint
EC	European Communities
ICJ	International Court of Justice
IDF	Israel Defense Forces
LSU	Logistical Support Unit
MFO	Multinational Force and Observers [in the Sinai]
OAU	Organization of African Unity
ONUC	Organisation des Nations Unies au Congo (United Nations Operations in the Congo).
OP	Observation Post
PLO	Palestine Liberation Organization
RDF	Rapid Deployment Force
SFM	Sinai Field Mission
SOP	Standing Operating Procedures
UNDOF	United Nations Disengagement Observer Force
UNEF-I	United Nations Emergency Force (1956-1967)
UNEF-II	United Nations Emergency Force (1974-1979)
UNFICYP	United Nations Force in Cyprus
UNIFIL	United Nations Interim Force in Lebanon
UNOGIL	United Nations Observer Group in Lebanon
UNTSO	United Nations Truce Supervision Organization
UNYOM	United Nations Yemen Observation Group

Selected Bibliography

Higgins, Rosalyn and Richard W. Nelson. United Nations Peacekeeping (London: Oxford University Press, 1985, forthcoming).

Homan, Cornelis, "MFO: Peacekeeping in the Middle East," Military Review, Vol. 63, No. 9 (Sept. 1983). Pp. 2-13.

James, Alan. "Symbol in Sinai: The Multinational Force and Observers." In H. Hanning, ed. Peacekeeping and Confidence-Building Measures in the Third World (N.Y.: International Peace Academy, 1985). Also: IPA Report (No. 20) 1985.

_____. _____. (Updated and slightly expanded version of the above). Millenium, Vol. 14, No. 3 (December 1985).

Lapidoth, Ruth. "The Multinational Force and Observers in the Sinai and Negev." In Gavriela Shalev, ed. Sefer Sussman (Jerusalem, 1984, Hebrew). Pp. 369-88.

Lucchini, Laurent. "La Force Internationale du Sinai: Le Maintien de la Paix sans l'O.N.U. "Annuaire Français de Droit International, Vol. 29 (1983). Pp. 121-36.

Nelson, Richard W. "Multinational Peacekeeping in the Middle East and the United Nations Model." International Affairs (London) Vol. 61, No. 1 (Winter 1984-85). Pp. 67-89.

_____. "Peacekeeping Aspects of the Egyptian-Israeli Peace Treaty and Consequences for United Nations Peacekeeping." Denver Journal of International Law and Policy, Vol. 10, No. 1 (Fall 1980). Pp. 113-53.

Pelcovits, Nathan A. Peacekeeping on Arab-Israeli Fronts: Lessons from the Sinai and Lebanon (SAIS Papers in International Affairs No. 3) (Westview Press/Foreign Policy Institute, School of Advanced International Studies, The John Hopkins University, 1984).

Pijpers, Alfred. "European Participation in the Sinai Peace-keeping Force (MFO)" In David Allen and Alfred Pijpers, eds. European Foreign Policy-Making and the Arab-Israeli Conflict (The Hague: Martinus Nijhoff, Publishers, 1984). Pp. 211-23.

174

Segal, David R., Jesse Harris, Joseph Rothberg and David Marlowe. "Paratroopers as Peacekeepers: U.S. Participation in the Sinai Constabulary Mission." A paper prepared for presentation at the 78th Annual Meeting of the American Sociological Association, Aug. 31-Sept. 4, 1983, Detroit, Michigan.

Thakur, Ramesh. "The Olive Branch Brigades: Peacekeeping in the Middle East." The World Today, Vol. 40, No. 3 (March 1984). Pp. 93-101.

Index